"This is a beautiful book. What a gem. *The Hidden Souls of Words* provides us with a precious key to a treasure we have often overlooked that lies hidden in the deep meaning of words. May we use it to unlock all kinds of power for the good of life."

— ARCHBISHOP DESMOND TUTU
Chair—Truth & Reconciliation Commission,
South Africa

"Words are ordinary things, with extraordinary power. Mary Garner has revealed a lot of that power in this wonderful book."

— MARIANNE WILLIAMSON
Author, *A Return to Love*

"*The Hidden Souls of Words* opens the window to the soul in order to awaken the dormant and hidden potential within us."

— DEEPAK CHOPRA
Author, *How To Know God*

"This book, *The Hidden Souls of Words* by Mary Garner, shares with us how valuable it is to learn about the understanding and meaning of words. There are many challenges we face in life and this book can be an inspiration to us all."

— SIR JOHN TEMPLETON
Author, *Discovering the Laws of Life*

"*The Hidden Souls of Words* is a marvelous book. It increases our knowledge of the deeper meaning of words and thus enables us to live in peace and happiness with one another."

— THE HON. ROBERT MULLER
Assistant Secretary General U.N. (retired)
Chancellor emeritus Peace University, Costa Rica
Author, *New Genesis—Shaping a Global Spirituality*

"Now comes an extremely useful and insightful book by Mary Garner called *The Hidden Souls of Words*—an A–Z collection of words, the origin, the meaning, and the impact of which author Garner explains with just the right touch, allowing us to 'see inside' these sounds and symbols and plumb from their depths the most effective use that we can make of them. More than this, however, Mary Garner uses her collection of words as a device to encourage us to ask some profound questions about our lives, and about life in General. It is in the tackling and the answering of these questions where much of the value of this book will no doubt be found."

— NEALE DONALD WALSCH
Author, *Conversations with God*

"Every crisis regardless of how small or large comes as a result of choosing the wrong words. *The Hidden Souls of Words* is not only a great catalyst for initiating more thoughtful dialogues that lead to actions, but also is a resource potential to help you heal the conflicts in your life."

— RABBI MICHAEL LERNER
Author, *Spirit Matters*

"The word is revealed in its lineage and meaning deepening our own understanding and connection with human history. *The Hidden Souls of Words* is a treasure to place next to your dictionary as a source of inspiration and contemplation."

— BARBARA MARX HUBBARD
Author, *Conscious Evolution*

"I find *The Hidden Souls of Words* to be a very thought provoking and soul searching book and give it my full endorsement."

— IFTEKHAR A. HAI
Director of Interfaith Relations
United Muslims of America

The Hidden Souls of Words

Keys to Transformation
Through the
Power of Words

MARY COX GARNER

SelectBooks, Inc.

This edition published by SelectBooks, Inc. For information
address SelectBooks, Inc., New York, New York.

First Edition

ISBN 1-59079-059-6

Library of Congress Cataloging-in-Publication Data
Garner, Mary Cox, 1937-
    The hidden souls of words : keys to transformation through the
power of words / Mary Cox Garner. -- 1st ed.
        p. cm.
Includes bibliographical references and index.
ISBN 1-59079-059-6 (hardcover : alk. paper)
    1. Language and languages—Religious aspects. 2. Spiritual life.
    I. Title.
BL65.L2G37   2004   210'.1'4--dc22
                                    2003026880

10 9 8 7 6 5 4 3 2 1

CONTENTS

ACKNOWLEDGMENTS

"Words are but empty thanks."

COLLEY CIBBES, 1671–1757

First and foremost, I want to express my gratitude to God for the ideas expressed in this book. I have received them as wonderful and unexpected gifts that came to me as if angelic messages, messages that continue to inspire me and to serve as guides for my life every day. The gift of such ideas affirms the reality of a universal Intelligence that is beyond our human comprehension which would not allow me to rest or be at peace until I wrote what became this book.

Innumerable kind hearts have contributed to this endeavor—would that I could acknowledge each one. Some are unknown because their words have become so much a part of me over a lifetime. Others are credited in the text of the book. As I think of all who have encouraged and sustained me, these words of Tennyson come to mind: "I am a part of all that I have met."

There are those special ones who have held my hand and stood beside me as the writing evolved. I shall name them alphabetically in lieu of a more creative plan to recognize and thank them:

Tom Bird—extraordinary, strong, insightful teacher who believed in me.

Sophy Burnham—who kindly read the manuscript and offered her invaluable guidance and encouragement..

Barbara Carpenter—intuitive spirit, loving friend and source of constant inspiration.

Bill Gladstone—enthusiastic, imaginative literary agent who loved this book from the beginning and who had faith in its publication.

Stephanie Ariel Marsh—without whose critical editorial work, computer skills, and personal support I could never have accomplished this project. Her sense of humor and intelligence made our creative collaboration a great joy.

The Hon. John McDonald—who made time to review and critique the manuscript. His suggestions were useful and appreciated.

Daniel Panner—kind and patient editor who brilliantly and gently guided me in amazing ways to make this a better book. He and Ariel helped me to recognize, understand, and appreciate the word support.

Kenzi Sugihara—Select Books publisher who had confidence in my work and who made it possible for the publication to become a reality.

And, finally, my husband Sanford Garner who upheld me through the process and who was always present as the unfailing, loving, secure, and wise anchor that he is.

My thanks and credit also to all those who challenged and encouraged me to write about the ideas we shared in the counseling sessions that facilitated their own spiritual journeys.

I am humbled and honored indeed by the generous endorsements given the book by Dr. Deepak Chopra; Iftekhar A. Hai, Director of Interfaith Relations, United Muslims of America; Barbara Marx Hubbard; Rabbi Michael Lerner; the Hon. Robert Muller; Sir John Templeton; Archbishop Desmond Tutu; Neale Donald Walsch; and Marianne Williamson.

For words, like nature, half reveal
And half conceal the Soul within.

—ALFRED LORD TENNYSON

I become aware of something in me that flashes
upon my reason, I perceive of it that it is something
but what it is I cannot see. It seems to me only, that,
if I could conceive it, I would comprehend all truth.

—MEISTER ECKHART

INTRODUCTION

Are you truly aware of the deeper meanings of the words that control your life?

A MATTER OF LIFE OR DEATH

All too often, we are unaware of the true meaning of the words that control our lives. The ineffective use and the misinterpretation of our God-given words have clouded our lives and caused great difficulty in our relationships. Communication is a deeply complex phenomenon. Adequate communication requires an openness of heart and spirit, coupled with a willingness to be patient, to listen carefully, and to seek to understand. Naturally, the choice of the appropriate words, with attention paid to inflection and tone while speaking them, is also of great importance. Effective communication requires the knowledge and understanding of cultural, intellectual, and educational differences that may exist in various situations and circumstances.

My tenure as an Arms Control and Disarmament negotiator made it crystal clear to me that it is essential to use words in a careful and correct way. All of us involved with those negotiations had to exercise extreme care in weighing and choosing every word, especially in talks with representatives of the then Soviet Union. Naturally, I had been speaking and writing words for almost my entire life, but in these negotiations, the effective use of words was literally a matter of life or death. Every word was of significant consequence. I came to realize this is always true, not only with regard to relationships between countries, but also between agencies within a country, each defending its own agenda and turf. In fact, the effective use of words is at the very root of our ability to live together in peace—in our own country, with other countries, in our communities, in our work lives, and especially in our homes and personal lives.

THE SOULS OF WORDS

The ancient Egyptians believed the human soul resided in the tongue, the "rudder" of the body. In my study of words, I have discovered that words themselves have souls, and that most of them share a deep spiritual source with the rest of life. Words are of ancient origin. In some instances, their origins are lost to us; in other cases, their forms and meanings evolved gradually as people moved about and began to explore every corner of the earth. In every case though, words have accumulated layers of meaning and nuance—that is part of what I mean when I refer to their "soul." Those layers always influence our communications whether we are aware of them or not. That is why it is so important that we try to come to understand them as deeply as we can. John Keats wrote, "Call the world if your please, The Vale of Soul Making. Then you will find out the use of the world."

This is much more than just a book about words. It is also not a book about etymology, even though in exploring each word I do mention its derivation. You will find that our language is a blending of many of the world's diverse languages, both past and present. For instance, you will see that the word "word" is derived from the Latin *verbum*, meaning the Divine Logos (the active Word of God), and also derived from the Indo-European word *werdh*, meaning to speak a word or sound. The soul of "word" therefore contains elements of Divine wisdom, light, and sound that are manifested in the world through human experience.

When we glimpse the soul of a word, our understanding of that word can also begin to change. For instance, once we recognize that the root of the word anger has to do with sorrow and grief, is it possible that our ways of dealing with anger could change? Would we be more likely to acknowledge and talk out our feelings without fear and shame, making use of the positive aspects of anger in our response to injustice and suffering in our world?

Or consider the example of the word competition. When you think of competition, what are your images and reactions? Most of us have forgotten that in its original sense competition was not only a struggle for supremacy, it also meant to act along with others—literally, "to seek together"—as each person contributed their special abilities in a joint effort. How would our world change if every person were to put the positive connotation of this word into action? We would compete only with ourselves to become more competent and to achieve our very highest and best possible.

These examples demonstrate that a deeper understanding of the souls of many everyday words will change your life dramatically, and change it now!

The words examined in this book have been arranged alphabetically under four headings—Communication, Enlightenment, Healing and Transformation. As I explored the soul of each word, the words appeared to fall naturally under one heading or another that seemed intuitively right to me. However, there isn't a brick wall between the words or the headings, for they constantly influence and nourish each other. The four categories in turn suggest the overall plan of the book—for as we explore the souls of the words and learn to communicate more deeply and effectively, this will lead to enlightenment. That enlightenment will in turn help us begin to undergo a healing which culminates in a transformation that is full of ongoing and never ending possibilities.

Effective communication is the essential ingredient in every part of our lives. True knowledge of the deeper meanings of words opens our hearts and spirits to communicate better with God and, therefore, with one another. On every level and in every aspect of life, our words are powerful and determinative, as *The Hidden Souls of Words* will make clear. Words can either create solutions and prevent many of the problems we face every day, or they can create more problems that are even worse. Aldous Huxley wrote, "Thanks to words, we have been able to rise above the brutes and thanks to words we have often sunk to the level of demons."

WORDS AND THE SPIRIT

While working with people who came to me for counseling and spiritual guidance, I was often asked to write down the thoughts I was expressing during our time together. I resisted this suggestion and hesitated for quite some time. Eventually, it became obvious there would be no peace in my heart until I surrendered to the writing process. It was surprising when the writings began to take the form of this book. My deepest gratitude goes out to the people who trusted me with a most precious part of themselves. In their quest to know themselves, the questions they raised were very revealing and gave me the clarity I needed to break down seemingly complex issues into the common elements that make up our human experience. It was an inspiration to me to witness their souls breaking old patterns and, when ready, making daring changes that moved their lives in new directions.

Words have played a critical role throughout my own spiritual development. My maternal grandmother exposed me to the power of words as a young, sensitive child. Thanks to her, I was memorizing verses of scripture as soon as I could speak. Many of these words have stayed with me until the present. This beginning launched me on a lifelong search for Truth. In college, that search ultimately led me to study the origin, interpretation, and meaning of words, with an in-depth focus on the history of various religious traditions and their literature. I began my first year of college armed with one of the most influential books of my life, *The Power of Positive Thinking*, by Norman Vincent Peale. I credit the powerful words in that book, along with the Prayer of St. Francis that my mother shared with me just before her death when I was sixteen, for giving me the attitude, vision, and courage necessary to begin important and new adventures, like college, or to persevere in the face of life's difficult obstacles and challenges.

Later in life, even through periods of agnosticism and skepticism, I returned to prayer again and again, and also continued the meaningful daily practice of quiet, transcendental meditation. However, intense inner struggles continued to plague me. Finally, my deep need for knowledge and insight led me in my despair to ask God for help, to guide me to some better way and teach me the Truth about prayer. Synchronistically a friend soon shared with me a remarkable work entitled *Effective Prayer*, by James V. Goure, a physicist and founder of United Research, Incorporated. This prayer made me aware of how unconscious I had been and helped me to rediscover the reality and power of my Divine Image or Creator presence (some call it Holy Spirit or Light). I then began to observe Light everywhere and in everyone, even in myself. As a result of this surrender, there was a marked change in my perspective; I attained a feeling of deep centeredness, and my attitude became one of profound gratitude. Feelings of depression, guilt, pain, loss, and grief that I had experienced in the past were gradually lifting and being positively transformed. Miracles soon began to happen as I sought to amend past mistakes and move into a place of forgiveness.

Gradually, I began to grasp that my prayer life was indeed my entire life, my every thought, word and action—my whole being. Our intentions are our true prayers, and they are fueled by the fire of our focused attention. Such a shift in perception and awakening can bring about what we call miracles. I reawakened to a longing that had stayed with me since I was a small child: I longed for every sentient being to be blessed with everything that love can bestow—not only the best of everything material in life, but also mental, emotional and spiritual well-being. This continues to be my heartfelt prayer every day.

When engaged in my counseling to assist others, I often shared this way of thinking of prayer. I discovered that those who were ready to see prayer in this way—and actually put it into practice—often took positive, new turns in their lives. At the same time, I also continued to learn and share through workshops, books and study. As a result, a renewing, healing Light continued to increase within me. I became aware that when we are ready, we can consciously participate in a creative, healing process that produces what we call miracles. I observed that those who seem to ignore, deny or close themselves off from this process were not making a choice to do so, as some believe. Rather, their experiences had not yet brought them to a level of consciousness that would allow an awakening and opening of their souls, which includes all of us to one degree or another. Until this awareness emerges, we tend to respond to life experiences from the unconscious reactive part of our psyche rather than from the conscious proactive and creative aspect of our nature.

Further, I concluded that we as human beings are all bound together through our souls. We are intricately linked and connected regardless of our separate ego/personalities and how they superficially interact one with the other. All of our experiences, and the words we use to describe them, are spiritual at their core. Author Phil Cousineau, longtime student and colleague of mythologist Joseph Campbell wrote, "The soul is the name for the unifying principle, power, or energy that is at the center of our being. To be in touch with soul means going back to the sacred source, the site of life-releasing energy, the activating force of life, the god-grounds."

HOW TO USE THIS BOOK

Are our words serving to bring about loving actions for ourselves and for others? Are we promoting a positive, creative spirit with the words we use, or are they taking us in an opposite unhappy or even destructive direction? This book is specifically designed to accentuate the former. Through an in depth understanding of the souls of the words we use day in and day out, *The Hidden Souls of Words* can enable people everywhere to have more peaceful and purposeful conversations; to enjoy more harmonious and meaningful relationships; and to face the dichotomies of life in a creative and healthy way.

This book can be used in different ways. You can approach it as a general, personal guide by reading a few pages every day, or you can refer to it when a question arises about the deeper meaning of a particular word in your life. The book is also structured in such a way that it can serve as a springboard for further thought and discussion with family, friends or colleagues.

After reading *The Hidden Souls of Words* we will never again be able to speak thoughtlessly or without careful attention and feeling. It will have given us a heightened awareness that our words are symbols of Divine wisdom given to assist us in our inextricable connection with God and one another. The spiritual truths for which so many are searching will be found or deepened as we look back to the roots or souls of these words. They will help us to be more responsible in the way we use all of our words, and all of our communications will be improved dramatically. The transformation of human relations, everywhere we are and wherever we go, is bound to be the natural result.

Turn this page, and let's change our lives and the lives of all those around us.

PART ONE

COMMUNICATION

Have you ever ordered something in a restaurant, even given special instructions to the waiter, and then found that the food you got was something completely different from what you had expected? If such a simple communication can go awry, imagine the possibilities for misunderstanding between corporations, institutions, communities, religions, governments, races, and even countries or nations.

In this section, we examine some of the elements that constitute real communication. The soul of communication includes words like friend, thought, and listen. Look further down the list and there are the words question, anger, imagine. Communication is not easy, and it's not always enjoyable, but it's always necessary. The necessity for effective communication at the international level is obvious. The United Nations is the instrument organized to promote and

9

negotiate peaceful exchanges between nations and people, but as we know so well, it can only be as effective as the willingness of the representatives involved to communicate and to share ideas expressed with words, then take action for the common good.

On a more personal level, have you ever noticed how a simple frown from the owner of a business can affect the employees? That frown, the result of an internal conversation in the mind of the employer, probably comes from a negative or unhappy nature. The power of even such unspoken words, expressed outwardly by the frown, often causes the employees to feel unappreciated or dissatisfied and thus become less productive.

The escalation of violence, both within the U.S. and abroad, can be attributed in no small degree to a breakdown in communication; to the way words are used; and to the unwillingness to communicate with words at all. What would have been different if the high school students who shot and killed their teachers and fellow students had been encouraged, before those horrible incidents, to communicate their frustrations or feelings to someone they trusted, be it parent, friend, or teacher (who would have really listened and heard their cries for help)? The same also holds true for the many who find themselves vulnerable to the dangers inherent in alcohol or drug use, since this is in essence a form of violence directed at oneself.

Civility and civilization depend on people everywhere understanding the impact of words and how to use them. Whether we are aware of it or not, all forms of communication—from silent thoughts to spoken words in all situations —influence others in either positive or negative ways.

anger

Anger is derived from the Medieval English, *angre* and the old Norse *angra*, meaning sorrow or distress, and also to grieve. The true or original soul of this word is very different from the connotation it often has.

Unexpressed emotions and needs can often bring about frustration, hurt, and disappointment. When we face our angry feelings openly and look deeply beneath the surface, they can help us to get in touch with the underlying sorrow and grief at their root. To contact the true essence of your angry feelings will require a probing, introspective look at the causes.

"For fear impoverishes always, while sorrow may enrich."
Alan Paton

Dr. Harville Hendrix, author of *Imago Relationship Therapy*, argues that the projection of what we hate about ourselves is unconscious and causes us to be angry at others until we begin to bring our projected self-hatred and accompanying sorrow to conscious awareness.

There is an appropriate and positive aspect to anger that we seldom acknowledge. As it helps us to be in touch with our sorrow and grief, anger can also motivate us to respond to injustices and suffering that we see around us in the world.

Martin Luther said, "I never work better than when I am inspired by anger."

Ralph Waldo Emerson wrote, "A good indignation brings out all one's powers."

However, most of us have been trained not to express or even acknowledge our anger. We have often been inappropriately taught to see anger as being "bad," yet when it is camouflaged it can make a difficult situation much worse.

Here are some examples of words we have been asked to live by:

Thomas Jefferson said, "When angry count ten before you speak; if very angry, a hundred."

Mark Twain humorously said, "When angry, count four; when very angry, swear."

There may be more wisdom in Twain's sense of humor than meets the eye. If it is possible to delay a reaction, it behooves us to look beneath our anger to see what other emotions it may be masking. However, this often entails having someone, a trusted person, to talk it over with.

Thomas Fuller said, "As fire kindled by bellows, so is anger by words."

"A soft answer turneth away wrath; but grievous words stir up anger." Proverbs 15:1

Another extreme danger can be in turning our anger inward and thus becoming depressed. Many have defined depression as 'anger turned inward,' as has cardiologist and author Dr. Dean Ornish, who describes how this can contribute to heart disease and other ailments. If this is so, there must be a great deal of unacknowledged anger in our society—after all, stress and heart disease are the leading causes of death, and depression permeates our society today.

The child psychologist Dr. Gail Gross describes how in her Judaic tradition the body is seen as a vessel that holds the light, the soul, or God. The three are equated and are understood as connecting everyone. When our light is obstructed by anger or by the repression of anger, what Carl Jung calls our 'shadow or disowned part,' we can either become ill or we project our insecurity and fears on others.

It has been confirmed and demonstrated that anger can dissipate once it is faced and talked out.

For instance, William Blake wrote, "I was angry with my friend, I told my wrath, my wrath did end. I was angry with my foe: I told it not, my wrath did grow."

Emily Dickinson said, "Anger as soon fed is dead, 'tis starving makes it fat."

How do you respond to feelings of anger? What are the symptoms of any anger you may have? Where has this anger originated? Look back at your life at your first recollection of a time of grief or sorrow. Do you think this could have led to repressed angry feelings? Think back to other moments when anger or even rage has stirred within you. Can you see that some of the emotions surrounding these incidents may have included sorrow, remorse, or grief? If you choose, allow yourself time to write what comes out when you reflect on these questions, asking the Creator within you to guide your insights. What deeper learning has come from your pain and suffering that you find revealed?

animals

The word animal is derived from the Latin, *anima* and *animus*, the same qualities of soul, or breath of life, as human beings.

The original meaning of the word makes it clear that animals are not, as the Cartesian view holds, creatures beneath the human order, but are wonderful and beautiful souls from a different and unique kingdom. Animals have not only provided companionship and help to mankind, but their very bodies have supplied the substance we have relied on to sustain our lives throughout history. Even today, many tribal cultures throughout the planet rely on their herds for food, clothing and shelter. Many societies still show their reverence for the animals they kill for food by giving thanks to God and also asking the animal's forgiveness for the taking of its life for nourishment.

This close bond with humans is demonstrated by the way certain animals can become part of our families as pets. They help us grow in our awareness of our mutual responsibility and interdependence.

How often has an animal brought joy into your life, nourished your spirit, or comforted you?

"Animals are such agreeable friends—they ask no questions, they pass no criticisms." George Eliot

Eugene O'Neill said in his *Dog's Will*, "Dogs are wiser than men. They do not set great store upon things. They do not waste their days hoarding property. They do not ruin their sleep worrying about how to keep the objects they have, and to obtain the objects they have not. There is nothing of value [they] have to bequeath except [their] love and [their] faith."

Walt Whitman wrote, "I think I could turn and live with the animals, they are so placid and self-contained."

"Of all God's creatures there is only one that cannot be made the slave of the lash. That one is the cat. If man could be crossed with the cat, it would improve man, but it would deteriorate the cat." Mark Twain

Henry Beston has written, "Animals shall not be measured by man. In a world older and more complete than ours, they move finished and complete, gifted with extensions of the senses we have lost or never attained, living by voices we shall never hear. They are not brethren; they are not underlings; they are other nations, caught with ourselves in the net of life and time, fellow prisoners of the splendor and travail of the earth."

Find a quiet space and think back to your first experience with an animal. How did you respond? What did this encounter or relationship mean in your life? What were your feelings? Were there qualities or insights that you felt you gained knowing or being with animals? What did they model for you? What would your life be like without animals?

art

The word art comes from the Latin *ars*, which means a way of being or of acting with innate skills or talents. The soul of this word implies that every person is born with some unique endowment; a special, gifted way of being and acting. Such a realization is contrary to our prevailing concept of the artist as a famous person who has been given some particular and extraordinary ability or capacity.

As Emile Zola said, "If you ask me what I came to do in this world, I, an artist, I will answer you: I am here to live out loud!"

Pablo Picasso must have recognized this when he said, "Every child is an artist. The problem is how to remain an artist once he grows up."

In the same vein, Henry James wrote, "Art is nothing more than the shadow of humanity."

Art has celebrated human creativity throughout history. Archeologists have been able to reconstruct much of ancient history from recovered artifacts, jewelry, clothing, buildings and sacred burial sites. The art of a culture is a signature that has helped historians track movements of civilizations from continent to continent. The most important aspect of art, whether from ancient or modern sources is, of course, the bridge it builds throughout time that lets us glimpse the soul of the artist and the people it represents.

There was a resurgence of all creative activities that came to fruition during the Renaissance period when cultures reawakened after the Dark Ages. Similarly, we as individuals can create our own personal Renaissance by nurturing our dreams, passions and inspirations.

The source of the word art clearly tells us that even though we may not recognize skills or talents within ourselves or in others, they are there. Further, these gifts take many forms, yet all art is mysteriously joined and speaks a language beyond words. It is easy to find this in the spaces between words in poetry, notes in music, lines in paintings, but it also lies within the spaces or creations of every soul in differing modes and formations.

Simonides wrote that, "Painting is silent poetry, and poetry is painting with the gift of speech."

Go back to the time when you first remember doing something artistic. Write or at least ponder about how you felt and what happened to you. Think back and remember the effect it had on you. What did it mean in your life then? Move forward to other times and to the present.

What inspiration have you received from art? Contemplate what art has done, and what it could do in the future. What is it that you feel passionate about, artistically? What are your talents and dreams? If you haven't acted on them, are you willing to overcome the fear that may be holding you back?

dance

Dance is derived from the old High German *damson*, to stretch out, and the Frankish *dintjan*, meaning to move here and there. To dance, therefore, is constant expansion, movement, and change.

We ordinarily think of dance in terms of physical movement, using our bodies in ballet, modern, or ballroom dancing at specific moments in time. However, the soul of this word implies that our whole being is involved when this stretching and constant movement takes place. The mind and spirit must be in harmony with our physical movement, for they are masterminding the energy flow required to dance.

"The dance is the highest symbol of life itself." Joseph Campbell

Dancing is one of the most primal instincts of mankind, coming only after the quest for food, water and shelter. Rhythm is the heart of dance and thus the heartbeat of life on earth. Before man was able to use speech effectively, body movements were used to communicate emotions and thoughts to others.

A monk was once asked about the theology of his tradition. He responded, "We have no theology, we dance." Scientists, along with many poets through the ages, use the metaphor of a gigantic dance to describe the constant movement and change taking place in the universe. In Hinduism,

18

Shiva is depicted as the Lord of the Dance, dancing in the flaming circle of creation and destruction, thus illustrating the frenzied dance of creation.

Sydney Carter wrote, "I danced in the morning when the world was begun...And I danced in the moon and the stars and the sun..."

"I have no desire to prove anything by dancing. I just dance." Fred Astaire

We are, in large measure, unaware of what the derivation of dance conveys as we witness all of the stretching, movement, and change always taking place around us. According to the accepted laws of nature, this motion is taking place in both the animate and what we call the inanimate at varying energy speeds. No thing and no one is excepted, and this makes our collective existence one that is inextricably unified and bonded.

What is the special dance that you, and only you, can uniquely perform? Are you aware of how much others depend on your particular dance and that it cannot be imitated or duplicated?

There are no wall flowers in the universal dance. We can choose to move in unison and harmony with the mystery of this dance, or listen to a different drummer, but it isn't possible to sit it out.

"The great end of life is not knowledge, but action." Thomas Fuller

Can you now see yourself as a minute, but important part of the cosmic dance of change? In what ways are your body, mind, and spirit moving to the beat and rhythm of the universe? Is there a balance that allows difficult moves to take place? Is the language of your soul being spoken in your life's dance?

friend

Friend is derived from the old English *freond*, meaning to love. The soul derivation of friend as a person who loves, or is loved, is no real mystery, for the thought of a friend as a loving person, or one easy to love and trust, is common to everyone.

When we acknowledge that God is the ultimate source of love within us, we will be less likely to look outside ourselves for someone or something to fill the void that we may feel. As we recognize the love inherent within ourselves, we become our own best friend and begin treating ourselves with tenderness, patience, leniency and love. Without this empowerment, we have no true love to share with a friend.

Eleanor Roosevelt said, "Friendship with oneself is all important, because without it one cannot be friends with anyone else."

When you recall and remember your friends and friendships, don't forget that they go hand-in-hand with freedom. Freedom is the essential ingredient in any relationship between those who love each other. The word friend is actually related to the word free.

"The most beautiful discovery true friends make is that they can grow separately without growing apart." Elizabeth Foley

Baltasar Gracian puts it succinctly when he writes that, "Friends are a second existence."

The mutual love and trust of our friends is a gift and treasure beyond description. It would be impossible to survive without friends! When I have the freedom to think 'out loud' with a trusted and trusting person, I have found a true friend.

"It is one of the blessings of old friends that you can afford to be stupid with them." Ralph Waldo Emerson

In today's technological society the cultivation of friendship can be a lost art. Many people today suffer from a lack of intimacy and rely on technology almost totally for their social interactions. How can we master the use of these electronic miracles? These tools need to be used to enhance our personal relationships rather than becoming a substitute for them.

Kipling describes real friendship as, "To each a man that knows his naked soul."

"Oh, the comfort, the inexpressible comfort of feeling safe with a person, having neither to weigh thoughts nor measure words, but pouring them all out, just as they are, chaff and grain together, certain that a faithful hand will take and sift them, keep what is worth keeping, and with a breath of kindness blow the rest away." Dinah Maria Mulock Craik

In what ways are you a true, loving friend to yourself? How deeply are you able to accept yourself, including all of your thoughts, feelings, and actions? Do you have a friend whom you can honor in this way? Do you honor one another's freedom? Are you a friend to someone else in the same way that you want to be befriended?

honesty

Honesty is derived from the old French *honeste* and the Latin *honestas*, meaning respectability. Honesty therefore implies thinking, speaking, and acting out of deep regard for both oneself and for others.

In what ways do you show a deep respect for yourself? Are you using the talents you have been given in self-satisfying ways that interest you? Are you relating to and dealing with others in ways that help them do the same?

"This above all; to thine own self to be true...thou cans't not then be false to any man." Shakespeare

We usually think of honesty simply as truth telling and abiding by law. Yet the soul of honesty reminds us that everything we say or do can either demonstrate respect for ourselves and others, or not.

"The most exhausting thing in life is being insincere." Anne M. Lindbergh

Sometimes we become dishonest when we are out of touch with our true feelings. This lack of honesty can result in feeling disconnected and lonely. When we have said or done what we consider to be dishonest, one way to restore our personal integrity and begin a process of self-forgiveness is to accept responsibility for our words and actions and, if feasible, to ask if there is anything we can do to make amends.

"The cruelest lies are often told in silence." Robert Louis Stevenson

In today's society, frankness, the expressing of one's personal opinions and judgments in casual social conversation, is often confused with honesty. This misleading interpretation is not worthy of the meaning of the soul of that word. This widespread misuse can cause pain and embarrassment and has little if anything to do with truth. When our thoughts, words and acts emanate from the soul of honesty, they will come from an enlightened deep respect and regard for ourselves and others. Armed with this knowledge, we can filter and if need be, disregard these frank and thinly veiled comments and when appropriate, help others understand this important distinction.

Sometimes expressing our feelings to others can result in discomfort for all parties. However, this action provides an opportunity to "clear the air" so that further dialogue may be more effective in resolving misunderstandings. When important issues are at stake, to ensure clear and effective communication, it is vital to convey your observations, understandings and desires to others for their consideration. Even information that may be difficult to convey can become much easier if we temper our words with love and kindness.

"There is only one corner of the universe you can be certain of improving, and that is our own self." Aldous Huxley

In the true sense of the root of the word, honesty with ourselves leads to honoring others, and honesty with others is an honoring of ourselves. If we were to truly live from this space how would the professional or business world transform? How would corporations change? Would the welfare of workers be balanced with the desire for profits? Would there be a trickle-down effect that would benefit the entire world's economy?

imagine

Imagine is derived from the late Latin *imago* and *imag-inare*, meaning to form an image of, in one's own mind or in the mind of another. Imagine is therefore what is happening now, in this very moment, as I write and as you read what I have written.

We usually think of imagination as the ability to make up something, often not realizing what influence our imaginative thoughts have on others. These thoughts fuel our actions and affect everyone around us. An important element of our life's process is the task of sorting through the images that our minds form.

"All acts performed in the world begin in the imagination." Barbara G. Harrison

We must not underestimate the world of unlimited creative possibilities within each of us through our imagination. To be able to imagine is one of the greatest and most important gifts of being human.

Theologian F. Thomas Trotter wrote, "To be able imaginatively to enter history is one of the great gifts of being human. It is the basis of all art and poetry and, in a special sense, history."

"Imagination is not a talent of some men, but is the health of every man." Ralph Waldo Emerson

We often admire and speak of the vivid and marvelous imaginations of children and longingly wish this quality would stay with us forever. In many ways it does. On the positive side, consider the marvels of the world that have come about because of imagination, coupled with our inventiveness. Without the ability to imagine, such wonders and unbelievable advancements would not have happened.

"A rock pile ceases to be a rock pile the moment a single man contemplates it, bearing within him the image of a cathedral." Antoine de Saint-Exupery

On the negative side, however, imagination is also responsible for the invention of weapons, war, and other means for destroying the planet and everything and every person on it. The human imagination can be misused to coerce, control, oppress, and enslave. There are far too many examples of such abuse in human history. We cannot take for granted the serious responsibility that goes hand in hand with our imagining capability. Truly this amazing and wonderful gift is awesome; both a treasure and a threat.

"There is no such thing as inevitable war. If war comes it will be from failure of human wisdom." Bonar Loa

The pros and cons of being able to imagine is another of life's major paradoxes.

We are bound together, and as we share in these powers of imagination anything can happen. If we can spend billions of dollars on armaments for defense, we should have the resources and desire to build a world of collective security based on a vision of loving interdependence.

"When there is no vision, people perish." Ralph Waldo Emerson

Think again about your ability to imagine. Can you see ways that it affects others and yourself as well? Imagine yourself using all of your talents to the best of your ability. How does this feel? Can you imagine everyone else doing the same with their lives?

joy

Joy is derived from the Latin *gaudia*, meaning to be in a state of gladness. Joy conveys an inner attitude of cheerfulness regardless of what may be occurring in one's life.

We usually associate joy with happiness that comes in certain moments. Yet the original root implies a constant state of mind or of being that is both a positive and empowering force. In the words of the Mundaka Upanishads:

"From joy springs all creation. By joy it is sustained, toward joy it proceeds, and to joy it returns."

"Man is that he might have joy." Joseph Smith

Is it possible that joy may be the primary energy that emanates from the Divine in order for the secondary energies of Light and Love to break forth as the building blocks of creation itself?

"We all carry within us: supreme strength, the fullness of wisdom, unquenchable joy. It is never thwarted and cannot be destroyed." Huston Smith

The ability to laugh, especially at ourselves and at the incongruities of life, is a mark of our humanity and likewise of God's image, or the Divine part of us. This can feed our souls and sometimes bring relief in tense moments. If joy is at the center of creation, it can create an attitude that reaches beyond happiness and helps us to stay centered while experiencing situations in which we might otherwise feel despair.

"The aim of spiritual life is to awaken a joyful freedom, a benevolent and compassionate heart in spite of everything." Jack Kornfield

To enjoy life is to be open to receive and thus be in the joy of the present moment. This often includes enjoyment of the simplest of gifts that life has to offer..

"It is not easy to find happiness in ourselves, and it is not possible to find it elsewhere." Agnes Repplier

Can joy enable us to live within the drama of our world, yet not be of it? Is that what Joseph Campbell means by "joyful participation in the suffering of the world"...and "the rapture of being fully alive"?

"We cannot cure the world of sorrows, but we can choose to live in joy." Bhagavad Gita

When was the last time you felt joy when you were not expecting it? What were the circumstances at that time? What do you think brought that surprising joy to you? What type of effect did it have on you? Think back to times when you were aware of a sense of joy in your life. Did it go beyond your life's circumstances? Did it arise from an inner state of being having more to do with your attitude? Is it possible that when we empty our minds of worldly concerns, only joy remains?

kind

Kind is derived from the Medieval English kin and the old English *cynn*, meaning kindred. The soul of kind thus implies a deeper relatedness than we ordinarily associate with acts of kindness or with kind feelings.

The original meaning of kind indicates that some of those who helped form and evolve the word must have experienced kindness as the natural, innate state of human beings, otherwise how would it have come into being and use? Words are invented to describe and communicate a feeling, a thought, or an experience. It is encouraging and helpful to know what kind tells us about how we are truly all one human family. How else could you explain your kind feelings or kindred spirit toward another?

"Kindness is the language which the deaf hear and the blind can see." Mark Twain

"Today I bent the truth to be kind, and I have no regret, for I am far surer of what is kind than I am of what is true." Robert Brault

Is there anything more loving than to feel deeply accepted, even with all of one's faults, by another person?

"Acceptance is the truest kinship with humanity." G.K. Chesterton

Many organizations around the globe now exist to further the understanding, importance and beauty of kindness as the primary consideration in daily living. This is an influential, hopeful and encouraging trend.

"Kindness in words creates confidence; kindness in thinking creates profoundness, kindness in feeling creates love." Lao-Tzu

"My religion is simple, my religion is kindness." The Dalai Llama

Think back to a time when unkind feelings came over you. What was happening? How did you react? Were you able to behave kindly in spite of those initial feelings? What happened in your life when others were unkind to you? What changes took place? How would human relations change in today's world if every person were educated to believe and accept what the soul of the word kind implies? Would the wall of separation eventually be broken, and deep, kindred, family-like relationship restored?

listen

L isten is derived from the archaic *list* and the Medieval
English *listen,* meaning to hearken. Listen is not just the
sense or act of hearing. The soul of this word calls us to pay
close attention not only to the words being spoken, but also
to their feeling tone and their deeper underlying meaning.

"We have two ears and one mouth that we may listen
more and talk less." Zeno

One way to test our listening skills is to focus on our
inner dialogue to see how deeply we are listening there. We
can observe and evaluate how the quality of our inner and
personal dialogue may be affecting our ability to listen. It
helps to get quiet and to practice this in order to connect at
a more profound level with those who speak to us.

"Listening is a magnetic and strange thing, a creative force.
The friends who listen to us are the ones we move toward, and
we want to sit in their radius. When we are listened to, it creates us, makes us unfold and expand." Karl Menninger

Lee Coit, author of *Listening. How to Increase Awareness of
Your Inner Guide,* says that we are listening to God's voice all
the time, whether we realize it or not. He gives several tips
for better listening and recommends setting aside a time
each day to listen and to write. As a part of this process, we
can allow thoughts to pass through the mind freely. This can
help to still one's mind and to let go of everything, except
the willingness or the desire to hear or listen. It also helps to

have confidence that God knows what is best for us and is both directing and guiding us in many different ways constantly. This Divine guidance can come through books, ideas, songs, our own writing, friends, even those not so friendly, and in numerous other ways.

We always know when we have heard the 'still small voice' of God's Spirit because we feel at peace deep inside. We can be assured that this inner voice will always speak from love and peace and will call us to change our perceptions in the best direction when we may feel confused.

"Be still and know that I am God." Psalm 46:10

"We are the wire, God is the current. Our only power is to let the current pass through us." Carlo Carretto

"The little child whispered, 'God, speak to me!' And a meadowlark sang. But the child did not hear. So the child yelled, 'God, speak to me!' And the thunder rolled across the sky. But the child did not listen. The child looked around and said, 'God, let me see you!' And a star shone brightly. But the child did not notice. And the child shouted, 'God, show me a miracle!' And a life was born. But the child did not know. So the child cried out in despair, 'Touch me, God, and let me know you are here!' Whereupon, God reached down and touched the child. But the child brushed the butterfly away and walked away unknowingly. Take time to listen. Often times, the things we seek are right underneath our noses. Don't miss out on your blessings because they are not packaged the way that you expect." Anonymous

Can you recall a time when you listened very well, or when you were listened to very well? What happened in your life as a result? Was there a healing or good feeling that came with that compassionate listening? Do you feel affirmed and valued when someone listens deeply and with understanding to you?

myth

Myth is derived from the Latin *mythus* and the Greek *muthos*, meaning a speech, narrative, or fable—and later, the adjective form *mythopoeic*, myth-making; combining myth with poetry. Myths, then, are formed to convey something meaningful; a story, often in a poetic or symbolic form.

We often think of myths as statements or stories that aren't really true. Yet the soul of myth conveys the possibility of profound truth told in the form of a fable created to express a significant experience. A preponderance of sacred writings fall into this category. These are too numerous to name, but if compared one with another, it is easy to see how they have built and borrowed myths from one another to express their unique wisdom. For instance, one can see how some Biblical stories were influenced by the dualistic religious system Zoroastrianism.

"A deep meaning often lies in old customs." Schiller

If we look deeply at mythology, we cannot miss the archetypes that continue to be relevant to our lives today. They are prototypes that can show standards for our lives to model. These patterns are examples and mirrors in both positive and negative ways. The ideas that come from mythology grew out of the experiences of humanity from the earliest civilization and they are an invariable part of our stories today.

Author Joseph Campbell writes, "Mythologies, in other words, mythologies and religions are great poems and, when recognized as such, point infallibly through things and events to the ubiquity of a 'presence' or 'eternity' that is whole and entire in each. In this function all mythologies, all great poetries, and all mystic traditions are in accord; and where any such inspiriting vision remains effective in a civilization, everything and every creature within its range is alive. The first condition, therefore, that any mythology must fulfill if it is to render life to modern lives is that of cleansing the doors of perception to the wonder, at once terrible and fascinating, of ourselves and of the universe of which we are the ears and eyes and the mind."

There are now abundant interpretations of important myths that lead to misguided teachings and actions - for example, violence and war in the name of religion. Look within the particular tradition that you personally embrace. Is it possible that most of the confusion we observe comes from literal translations of sacred writings, or from the lack of awareness that they were not meant to be interpreted only as historical documents?

"Frequently a symbol doesn't open our eyes, but closes them instead. If we concretize the symbol we get stuck with it." Joseph Campbell

Is it possible that scriptures contain spiritually revealed truths presented in the form of myths, pointing to or attempting to connect us with the consciousness of our God presence?

"A true symbol takes us to the center of the circle, not to another point on the circumference. It is by symbolism that man enters effectively and consciously into contact with his own deepest self, with other men, and with God...." Thomas Merton

"The divine manifestation is ubiquitous, only our eyes are not open to it." Joseph Campbell

When interpretation of a myth confuses or eludes you, look again at the message it is trying to deliver, to determine if there is a universal truth in it that you may apply or use meaningfully. If we look deeply, mythology reveals evidence that the One power beckons to us to experience the infinite in our lives?

photograph

Photo is derived from the Greek *phos*, meaning light, and from the Greek *graphein*, meaning to write. Photography is thus like writing with light.

This description of photographs reminds us of how they are similar to writings, for they both enlighten our thoughts and ideas and show the truth of a moment in time. They bring all of our senses to bear, the senses that make us human beings.

"The sound stops short the sense flows on." Old Chinese saying

Cameras existed long before photographs were invented. In ancient times, the *camera obscuras* was a light-capturing device that used a pinhole to project images on walls in darkened rooms. In the 16th and 17th centuries, this device was improved by enlarging the hole and inserting the lens of a telescope and used primarily by artists who could trace the images to create the first drawings with exacting perspective.

As we look at each photo, feelings such as love, happiness, sadness, fear, or grief can be awakened from past memories. They can even bring about a new awareness that we have never experienced before.

Some photographs touch us deeply, while others are meaningless to us. Whether we like what we see or not, photos capture what is in the 'now' of that moment. They reflect choices that were made to record and preserve an experience, and each has its own special meaning.

"Great art is an instant arrested in history." Huneker

With the advent of digital photography, pictures can be altered and even created virtually from thin air, and it is possible for these images to have no real basis in the objective world. These created pictures have their origin in the imagination and are taking the art to new and exciting horizons.

How has the advent of photography impacted the depth of our historical records?

Think of a photograph that recently attracted you. Why did it touch you? In what way(s) did it touch and interest you?

prayer

Prayer is derived from the Latin *precari*, meaning to request or ask, which is the common understanding or use of the word. Later, however, the meaning shifted from asking or seeking to the notion of prayer being a loving attitude.

Now, the word refers both to a petition and to an opening to the experience of Divine love. Thus, the soul of the word prayer confirms that praying and love go hand in hand.

In the context of the soul of this word, every thought we think, every feeling we have, every word we utter, every action we take, regardless of how inconsequential we consider them to be, is a powerful prayer. Thus, we are in a state of constant prayer.

"Prayer moves the hand that moves the world." John Aikman Wallace

"Prayer is not an exercise, it is the life. The purpose of prayer is to reveal the presence of God equally present, all the time and in every condition." Oswald Chambers

There are as many methods, modes, and interpretations of prayer as there are individuals and their faiths or spiritual traditions. Through the ages, mankind has felt a driving need to connect to the Creator, both by what we call 'going within ourselves' and by a variety of outward worship practices.

"Prayer is and remains always a native and deepest impulse of the soul of man." Thomas Carlyle

"The deepest wishes of the heart find expression in secret prayer." George E. Rees

There is no one or right way to pray. Prayer may consist of praise, confession, thanksgiving, intercession, petition, acts of service, chanting, silence, various forms of meditation, guided visualization, or simply being, listening, feeling, centering, thinking, or doing. Whatever the method, there are results.

Cardiologist Randolph Byrd has shown that prayer can be a powerful force for healing. He conducted a rigidly controlled scientific study on the effects of prayer. Dr. Byrd demonstrated by the successful recovery rate of his patients who had been prayed for three times a week that human consciousness does extend beyond one's body through loving prayer. Those who prayed for the patients used whatever method of prayer they wanted. Dr. Bryd commented that this study confirmed that we have what he called a 'nonlocal' aspect to our being in space and time, which we share with the Divine.

Scientist Greg Braden writes about a lost mode of prayer that transcends what we think of as "religious prayers." Braden links the scientific world of quantum physics with what he calls a "technology of prayer." This form of prayer relies on human emotion, or a "force" in humans, that can change outer reality. The Essenes, an ancient Jewish mystical sect, were the originators of this wisdom, which combined the direction of thought and the power of emotion to create the feelings they experienced as their 'real' prayers.

Other studies have shown that nondirective prayers, with focused attention and without attachment to a specific result, are amazingly effective. Ingenious attempts to objectively assess the effectiveness of various ways and forms of praying have been quietly undertaken by the organization

Spindrift. In one of their tests, they found that prayer is more powerful when a "Thy will be done" approach is used rather than when a specific goal or result is held in the mind.

Dr. Larry Dossey said, "Although both methods were shown to work, the non-directed technique appeared quantitatively much more effective, frequently yielding results that were twice as great or more when compared to the directed approach. The Spindrift experimenters are aware of the scientific heresy implied by their findings. 'Scientifically,' they state, 'it is a shocking thing to think of 'force' as intelligent, loving, kind, good, and aware of needs."

Have you ever considered that there might be a prayer that could bring a negative result such as worry? Some even define worry as praying for what we do not want.

"I have lived to thank God that all my prayers have not been answered." Jean Ingelow

Modern science validates a causal relationship between our thoughts, feelings and dreams and the world at large. Perhaps what happens in every moment that we engage another person or a situation is what matters most. Deepak Chopra says that our "hearts cross talk" and our souls have a collective heart beat which broadcasts a subtle exchange of information that is beyond space and time.

"The very best and utmost attainment in this life is to remain still and let God act and speak in thee." Meister Eckhart

Those who begin their day with prayer or meditation time, in whatever form, report that they can project a more peaceful presence throughout the day. In addition, when the prayer/meditation practice becomes habitual, they notice that people respond to them in a more positive way as a result.

It helps to remember that the whole of our life's expression is that of a continuous prayer.

When and how do you pray? What does prayer mean to your life? Are you aware of the influence that everything you think, say, and do has on others? Have you allowed the Divine inspiration you receive through prayer to guide your life? If not, are you willing to try now?

question

Question is derived from the Latin *quaere*, meaning to seek or to ask, and from the late Latin *quaestionarius*, meaning a judicial inquisitor exacting answers. Question, or querying, thus refers not only to our common use of the word, the seeking of information, but also to the possibility of a painful process of extracting answers.

Sometimes, as the soul of the word indicates, questions may feel like an inquisition, rather than an inquiry. At times, those around us become very uncomfortable and even fearful when we ask questions. Before we pose a personal question to someone, we need to be sensitive to the individual's need for privacy and remember to respect personal boundaries.

"It often takes more courage to change one's opinion than to stick to it." Georg Christoph Lictenberg

Do you find you have spent most of your life questioning and seeking answers? Hidden beneath every question may be a longing to know the truth about our human nature and existence.

"It is not every question that deserves an answer." Publilius

"Any path is only a path, and there is no affront, to oneself or to others, in dropping it if that is what your heart tells you." Carlos Castaneda

This intensive search can take us down many paths. For many, these paths have included schools, advanced degrees, job searches, professional positions, numerous workshops and study courses through which they hope to find the right or missing piece for their puzzling questions.

"Progress is impossible without change, and those who cannot change their minds cannot change anything." George Bernard Shaw

The next time you fear asking questions, remember that others have asked the same or similar questions through the ages, and that these questions contain gifts necessary to progress. They move us to stay connected to our deepest and most important values. There are no trivial questions.

"The most fatal illusion is the settled point of view. Since life is growth and motion, a fixed point of view kills anybody who has one." Brooke Atkinson

While continuing to search for truth from the world, can you at the same time search within yourself to evaluate the value and integrity of that information?

"Truth is not introduced into the individual from without, but was within him all the time." Soren Kierkegaard

"In questioning, go deep. In seeking truth, explore everything. Do not be satisfied with finding truth: Once one has found truth, the real danger begins. Once one becomes convinced and certain, the real danger begins. Once one becomes right, the nightmare begins. It is not necessary to find truth, only seek truth. The seeking keeps us flexible, fluid, and free—permeable to life's infinite mystery and beauty." Robert Rabbin

What questions have been most prevalent in your mind throughout the majority of your life? In what way have they posed themselves? Is there any commonality among them? How can you integrate new truths and insights that may develop into your ongoing spiritual practices?

scripture

Scripture is derived from the Latin, *scriptio*, meaning scribe. The inference is that scripture is written by human beings.

Many strongly believe that scripture was handed or dictated to humans by God, yet, as seen from the soul of this word, scripture was from earliest times understood to be the work of human scribes or writers. It is a form of poetic writing that was and continues to be a symbolic means for the expression and transmission of Divine inspiration and revelation.

Most people today do not know they have the gift of inspired writing. They have been told that only certain extraordinary gurus, sages, seers, or scribes of holy literature, who wrote in the distant past, could write in such a manner. Have we so separated ourselves from God that it is impossible to believe that inspired revelation could come through us today, or that further revelation is even needed?

The literal interpretation of many of the ancient "Holy Books" has been used by some people as an excuse for the perpetration of all kinds of horrors: cruelty, oppression and repression, slavery, prejudice, murder, violence of every variety, and war, to name only a few examples. All we have to do is look at all sources of religious scriptures to find illustration after illustration that, if taken literally, incite crimes against humanity and civilization, under the guise of the purging of evil.

"Men have misused Scripture just as they misuse light and food." Frederick William Farrar

The enlightened purpose of most scripture is to draw us to the Spirit of God, the source that gives us life and freedom. However, it is often interpreted as the literal letter of the Law which binds, enslaves, and takes life away. Such concealment or alteration of the original intrinsic spiritual meaning of scripture has fueled disastrous divisions, violence, and wars and often veiled the higher aspirations that each religion meant to create and foster. Extremists of all persuasions are well known living examples of this literalism and misinformation.

In September 2003, Noga Tarnopolsky, a columnist for the *Washington Post* wrote, "In Jerusalem, words mean *nothing* and *everything.*"

"Talking about God is not at all the same thing as experiencing God or acting out God through our lives." Philip Hewett

Are our actions something that the God we profess to believe in would condone? Is it possible that these misunderstandings of the "Holy Word" can be remedied?

If we consider the context and original, deep meanings of the words of the various scriptures, as well as the cultures that created them, would this help bring more harmony and peace in the world? Is it what the holy books say that is the issue, or is it what interpreters say the words say that is at issue? Isn't it all right to have differing opinions about what scripture means, without making others wrong or even denying their right to exist?

Have we forgotten that even though Divinely inspired, all sacred books were written by human hands and therefore modified by interpretations? Can you entertain the possibility that you can yourself receive revelatory inspiration that is relevant to today?

Have you ever written anything that you felt was inspired? Are you willing to ask for revelatory inspiration and to listen for Divine guidance now?

television

Television is derived from the Greek *tele*, meaning to see far off, and from the Latin *vide*, meaning vision. The soul of this word thus refers to what we visualize, rather than the commonly held idea that TV is whatever others put before us on a screen.

"All television is educational television. The question is: what is it teaching?" Nicholas Johnson

So much human creative genius has gone into the production of technology. This technology, in combination with the science of electronics, has allowed us to put pictures on to the silver screen, television, computers, and now even cellular telephones. Many years ago movies were called picture shows. Television, videos, movies, etc., are created by the media and production companies for the viewing public, yet we have the all important power of choice to make decisions about what we choose to view.

"Television is the first truly democratic culture—the first culture available to everybody and entirely governed by what the people want. The most terrifying thing is what people do want." Clive Barnes

So many images that are screened today are unreal, but made to appear real, which is a major problem of mind and spirit for all ages. What kind of truth and reality do we want in our lives? This is an essential question everyone must ask and parents must answer on behalf of their children too young to answer for themselves.

"When television is good, nothing is better. But when television is bad, nothing is worse." Newton Minnow

A new scientific study has found that boys and girls who see violence on television have a heightened risk of aggressive adult behavior, including spousal abuse and criminal offenses, no matter how they act in childhood. Psychologist L. Rowell Huesmann at the University of Michigan's Institute for Social Research said televised violence suggests to young children that aggression is appropriate in some situations. It also erodes a natural aversion to violence. He recommends that parents restrict viewing of violent TV and movies by young children and preteens as much as possible.

"In the age of television, image becomes more important than substance." S.I. Hayakawa

The Washington, DC-based Institute for Mental Health Initiatives is a pioneer organization that works with the media to visualize positive role modeling in broadcast productions, and it has given recognition awards to those who have succeeded in attaining this goal. IMHI has also entered a joint project with the public TV media to air public service announcements geared to children and adults focused on the channeling of anger. A resulting spin-off from these programmed announcements is an educational video and curriculum on 'Anger Management' that is currently being used by some public schools.

The human race is facing a critical moment of decision about what we want to 'picture' our world and society to be like and what we choose to promulgate. Have we forgotten that we have been given dominion over the earth? Have we also forgotten that this dominion does not mean exploitation?

It means that we are responsible for the care and nurture of all the earth and its kingdoms, including our young minds.

"He who prides himself on giving what he thinks the public wants is often creating a fictitious demand for low standards which he will then satisfy." Lord Reith

"The television commercial is the most efficient power-packed capsule of education that appears anywhere on TV." C.L. Gray

We hear again and again that "a picture is worth a thousand words"; however, both pictures and words are even more powerful when combined to give a positive message. Do you ever wonder if the world scene and our lives, as shown and commented on via our television screens, are being influenced in any positive, redeeming way by the vision and level of current TV programming, or other similar technologies? If not, why not? Have we given in to poor taste, cynicism, questionable values, and to 'what sells, shows'? Are you even aware of the fact that you have the power and the responsibility to create your own positive images?

Think of a time when you were impacted by television. What influence did it have on you? Was it life enhancing and positive, even relaxing, or did it have the opposite effect? Are you satisfied or pleased with television programming as it is today?

thought

Thought is derived from the old English, *thence,* and from the old Norse, *thekkia,* meaning to know. Related to this derivation is the old English, *thakancian,* which became to thank or to express a grateful thought, or to receive a gift with gratitude. The soul of the word thought, then, tells us that it is equated with gratitude for an "inner knowing" or the gift of "awareness;" this is an expansion of what we typically mean by the word thought. It is more than merely the faculty of reason.

Early on, those who were inventing words must have been aware of the existence of an amazing and creative Universal Intelligence, inner knowing, or awareness that can become operative in our thoughts. This creative force that can inspire thought is everyone's gift from God, and the power of it is very humbling. It is an innate gift or energy that is both a part of us, and a mystery that is beyond us. Even though we cannot comprehend its origin, we can observe its creative manifestation working in us and through us as a consciousness that can direct our wills and thus our world. We have the freedom to conduct creative responses in concert with that Divine impetus.

"Life is a mirror and will reflect back to the thinker what he thinks into it." Ernest Holmes

Part of thought is God's gift of reason, which allows us to estimate the consequences of our actions. We have the freedom to use this creative energy to manifest negative, fearful thought forms that can even be projected globally. This is called mass consciousness, and it is created by the many who are still arrested at the purely physical and unconscious levels of being, rather than at a more conscious, elevated, heart-centered level. This higher expression allows Divine loving guidance to reveal itself. What would the world be like if materialistic minds were to be put at the service of a transcendent, guiding force as they were intended to be? Would this powerful, heart-centered energy then govern and guide all our relationships and actions? What if mass consciousness awakened to this end?

"The world is a great mirror. It reflects back to you what you are. If you are loving, if you are friendly, if you are helpful, the world will prove loving and friendly and helpful to you. The world is what you are." Thomas Dreier

If we observe or pay close attention to our thoughts, can we see that they may in reality be forms of prayer that account for our role in making the circumstances of our lives what they are?

"Great men are they who see that the spiritual is stronger than any material force, that thoughts rule the world." Ralph Waldo Emerson

"Happiness is when what you think, what you say, and what you do are in harmony." Mahatma Gandhi

We may not be aware of how our thought energies affect others, but it has been shown that thoughts can influence anything or anyone instantaneously.

The following came to me in a vivid dream. While sitting in a circle—looking at people in the circle—I saw that some were being judged for not having any special gifts. The inner message of the dream was that our thoughts and feelings are so powerful that they can either call forth the inner gifts of people, or cause them to remain blocked or hidden within them. Further, for the world to realize its highest potential and be what it was originally intended to be, all God-given talents, even if tiny seeds, need to be nourished in everyone.

Our thoughts can be like angels or demons according to the way we use them.

Browning recognized and acknowledged the power of thought when he wrote,

"Thought is the soul of action."

Our thoughts can be the soul of inspiration as well.

"The thoughts that come often unsought, and as it were, drop into the mind, are commonly the most valuable of any we have." John Locke

Locke wrote those words long before we coined the term "creative visualization," which is the power to make something happen by our focused thought.

"What you think about and thank about, you bring about." John F. DeMartini

These words came on a card along with a birthday gift that I received from my son. It was a small blue stone with the word Light inscribed on the face. It was called a magic stone to be used for centering, prayer, or meditation; by thinking or talking about the word 'Light' carved on the stone, that quality would soon become manifest. I call it "my miracle stone," and often share the positive light energy I receive from it with others. I try to visualize the Light as being present everywhere and glowing in everyone, especially when on the surface it is not at all apparent. My son knew that I had been practicing this for years through a "Light Prayer," and I was deeply touched that he remembered in such a special and specific way with his gift.

"The power of thought is the magic of the mind." Byron

One of the books that has influenced millions and continues to be helpful today is *The Power of Positive Thinking*, by Norman Vincent Peale. I often remember his words: "Change your thoughts and you change your world."

Have you ever been aware of the effect and impact of your thoughts on others? If so, what was the result? Are you willing to be more aware of how your thoughts influence others in the future?

word

Word is derived from the Latin, *verbum*, meaning the Divine Logos (the active Word of God), and from the Indo-European, *werdth*, or *iver*, meaning to speak a word or sound. The soul of word refers therefore to Divine wisdom, light, and sound that manifests in the world through human experience.

Antisthenes said, "The investigation of the meaning of words is the beginning of education."

Do you use words without consciously thinking of the Divine power they have? The derivation of word confirms that words are active, evolving symbols of our thoughts, our prayers, our internal conversations with the Divine. According to the soul of this word, all words are God given gifts in their creation and meant to be used for the benefit of all.

"In the beginning there was the Word and the Word was with God and the Word was God." John 1:1

It is interesting to observe how our words, feelings, or thoughts actually manifest as real events in our lives. Some of these connections are obvious, but others take time and retrospection in order for us to comprehend the profound impact that words have on the world around us. Whether spoken, unspoken, or written in all languages, words are proclamations of what is true for us. Words affirm our intentions.

"The tongue has the power of life and death." Proverbs 18:21

When Henry Ford was a young man, Thomas Edison said to him, "You've got it!" when referring to Ford's idea of a vehicle that contains its own fuel. Those encouraging words were so commanding that they inspired Ford to develop the automobile. While the automobile revolutionized the world, the human tongue, together with the human voice, is the most powerful vehicle ever created.

"The word is not just a sound or a written symbol. The word is a force; it is the power you have to express and communicate, to think, and thereby to create the events in your life. The word is the most powerful tool you have as a human; it is the tool of magic." Don Miguel Ruiz

The words that are a part of the self talk that goes on in our minds send out messages far and wide. Their energy affects the outer world in invisible ways that we may never know about.

"Since the concepts people live by are derived only from perceptions and from language and since the perceptions are received and interpreted only in light of earlier concepts, man comes pretty close to living in a house that language built." Russell R. W. Smith

We do not know exactly when languages evolved, but there are 6,300 of them in existence in the world today. The repetition of practices and traditions (*memes*) that come from the languages that have survived shape our minds and cultures; these practices drive the evolution of ideas and breakthroughs, and accumulate like genes. Communities were formed through the use of words to share information, have conversations, and negotiate social relationships.

"Speech is civilization itself. The word, even the most contradictory word, preserves contact—it is silence which isolates." Thomas Mann

In a sense, spoken words are always fractional finite artic-ulations—interpretations that emanate from an unfath-omable sacred silence. The frequencies transmitted from the words we speak cannot be retrieved. They tell us how we truly feel about ourselves. The more loving and honest our words, the more they demonstrate our own self-respect. The way we speak about others reflects the way we feel about ourselves, which may be hidden from our everyday awareness or consciousness.

"Speech is a mirror of the soul: as a man speaks, so is he." Publilius Syrus: Maxim

When the Buddha taught the Eightfold Path in order to help us become free of suffering, he spoke concerning the use of words in our daily speech and suggested we consider whether or not our words are true and if they are useful. This important daily practice may be difficult to remember in our offhand conversations, but it can be a way of retrain-ing our tendency to respond or to react instantly and with-out thinking, in the midst of a fast paced life.

Our words have the power to create community, loving relationships, and connections among people, but they also have the ability to cause divisions and even destruction. Recall the frightful and inciting words of Adolph Hitler and the unbelievable holocaust that resulted.

"All the magic you possess is based on your word. Your word is pure magic, and misuse of your word is black magic." Don Miguel Ruiz

How have the powerful words of others influenced your life? Who spoke them and what did they say? Think of a time when your words, together with the feelings under-neath them, had a positive effect on someone else. What words did you use and what was the result? Can you be more aware in the future of how the words you use affect others?

write

Write is derived from the old English Anglo-Saxon *writan*, meaning to carve or scratch symbols, and from the Latin *scribere* or *scribe*, which first meant to 'dig in,' rather than to mark on the surface. The soul of write refers not only to the symbols we use, but also implies both the inspiration and the recording of our thoughts.

The Dutch writer Harry Mulisch in his book *The Discovery of Heaven* said that, "Life is ultimately reading."

For some, life is also writing, for writing allows us to access a deeper part of ourselves and helps us attempt to say what is sometimes unsayable, as the root word implies. We often write in order to grow in the awareness and understanding of our own feelings and thoughts, and to better express them. This can be a step toward mastery of those feelings and thoughts as well.

"I think with my right hand." Edmund Wilson

Writing helps us to quiet our minds on paper. As we allow ourselves the freedom of expression, an innate wisdom is accessed that is often surprising and inspiring. When we consciously call on the Creator to be our guide, there is no end to the discoveries that are available.

"The act of writing is the act of discovering what you believe." David Hare

"Nothing you write, if you hope to be any good, will ever come out as you first hoped." Lillian Hellman

The process of writing slows down our minds, helps us focus and allows what lies in the quietude of our being to be revealed in the form of words. From the depth of silence in God's presence come unlimited gifts of peaceful inspiration. Through writing, our souls speak to us of our hidden, innermost thoughts that when shared with others are more than mere words; they express the essence and beauty from the most profound part of ourselves.

"You have to throw yourself away when you write." Maxwell Perkins

A concrete example of the powerful value of writing is demonstrated by the nonprofit literary publication, *Journal of Ordinary Thought,* founded by Professor of Education Hal Adams from the University of Illinois. He began publishing under the slogan, "Every person is a philosopher" in 1996. The storytellers and poets include people from all walks of life ranging from college students to convicts, janitors to CEOs. Many report that having their literary reflections taken seriously eases their sense of isolation, increases their confidence and helps to bring order to their lives. Recently, the use of therapeutic writing and workshops has become a popular tool used by social service agencies.

James Pennebaker, a psychologist at the University of Texas, discovered from the data of a scientific study that those who drew on their deepest feelings and wrote about their most traumatic experiences eventually had fewer doctor's visits, better immune system functioning, lower stress, and various other social and cognitive benefits. This finding makes clear that every person could benefit from writing. Many who already keep a journal have found how therapeutic it can be.

By the time we have written words, we will be a different person. It happens with each stroke of the pen. Such constant change can make us ambivalent about writing, because in the next moment we may have a new thought or want to write the prior thought in an entirely different way. This concern can cause us to hesitate to make our writing public.

"How can I know what I think until I see what I say." E.M. Forster

In addition, writing makes us aware that there are no new ideas, just other ways of expressing what Deepak Chopra calls "recycled information."

"There is no new thing under the sun." Ecclesiastes 1:9

"Nothing is said which has not been said before." Terence

"I quote others in order to better express my own self." Montaigne

Recall the last time you wrote about something or to someone. Did it draw you to a place of inner quiet? What was revealed to you during the course of the writing that you had not thought of before, or in that particular way? Will you use writing more in the future as a means to listen quietly to God, collect your thoughts, express your inspirations, and empower your life?

PART TWO

ENLIGHTENMENT

"Let there be light."

They are the oldest words in the universe—older even than the universe; in a sense, they are the words that called the universe into being. Yet after countless millennia, this simple phrase remains the fundamental prayer of all people everywhere, whatever their faith. This book is concerned with the hidden souls of words, and in the case of enlightenment, we have an instance of a word with a soul of unimaginable resonance and power. Over the course of human history, the quest for enlightenment has taken many shapes and been called by many names. Enlightenment is a concept that by its nature embraces opposites and reconciles paradoxes. Look over the list of words discussed in this section. Some are what you would probably expect: love, light, education, and peace. All of these are certainly embedded in the nature of enlightenment. But look again.

Competition. Illusion. Isolation. Human. Are these words that you would normally associate with enlightenment? Perhaps the word that unifies the whole section is one that appropriately is located at its center—Mystery. Light surrounds us, but none of us can grasp it in our hands.

The opening section of this book examined the idea of communication, and while communication is essential, as we all know, it can be difficult as well. What we have to communicate is not always affable. Similarly, it is not always easy or pleasant to achieve enlightenment—the wisdom gained on the path to enlightenment is often fraught with pain. No one is immune. Life contains suffering as well as joy, and competition and isolation are elements of everyone's experience. But enlightenment means more than just opening up to the truth. When we fully open ourselves to the awareness of the absolute light that is powerfully connected to us, then we can begin to lighten our burden—literally, 'enlighten' ourselves—in a way that makes true peace possible.

competition

Competition is derived from the Latin *competere*, meaning to meet the requirements, also, to seek together. Competition conveys both a need to meet standards and to do so along with others.

"The whole world seems to teach us to be competitive, but the real reason for all this competition is the desire for love." James Goure

Over and over again we are told that competition is the motivating force at the heart and nerve center of our society. There is certainly a positive side to the competitive spirit which calls forth a strong effort to be our 'best' and to 'achieve.' At the same time, there is often a negative result, occurring within us and around us, in the attempt to live up to a standard set by others that can make us feel inadequate, insufficient or at times even worthless. Such misinterpretation of the soul meaning of competition permeates our culture.

Sometimes a harmful battle brews out of this activity of making comparisons between 'them' and 'us'; judgments that tell us we are 'good' or 'bad'; or in striving to 'win' at all costs. Are the negative happenings in the world around us, like greedy and corrupt corporate practices, cheating on examinations, the violence that erupts at sporting events, and even genocide, the direct results of frenzied competition? Unfortunately, this negative energy or attitude that often accompanies the distorted view of competition is passed on to our children. From it, they learn to fear that there is not enough of anything in life to go around.

Competition is fostered by a desperate desire for love and approval. Those who misunderstand competition are simply unaware that the Source of a Divine unlimited supply of love is within each one of us, and that we never again have to seek for love from anyone or anything. In fact, when we realize that this expression of love is something different from what we normally think of as human love, we can share this gift of love that is always present.

Jean Vanier says that, "Envy comes from people's ignorance of, or lack of belief in, their own gifts."

The person that we are meant to compete against, according to the soul of the word competition, is ourselves. There is no need for 'winners' or 'losers' when everyone is seeking together. Then, everyone wins, even at so-called competitive events. Most of us have never really known that the derivation of the word competition originally meant to not only meet requirements, but to do so along with others; to seek together, not to dominate, but to bring out one another's gifts.

True leaders and bosses in the workplace are those who encourage both teamwork and the development of each worker's special abilities by showing genuine appreciation and respect for each person's valuable contributions.

The world will be quite a different place when we learn to emphasize and act out the positive spirit of the soul of competition—a society in which each person would only compete with 'themselves' to become competent and the best they could possibly be in their own right.

George Herbert said that, "Skill and confidence are an unconquered army," and Francis Bacon wrote that,

"Natural abilities are like natural plants, that need pruning by study."

How does the spirit of competition as now practiced affect your life and our world today? How does the force of competition affect your ability to live and work with others? Write down, or at least think about, how you define and how you feel about competition. How do you think this true definition of competition will improve your life?

connection

Connection is derived from the Latin *connectere*, meaning linked together. Implicit in the word is the idea that everything in creation and life is related to everything else.

Contrary to the way we ordinarily define connection, as something separated that temporarily relates or fastens to someone or something, the soul of the word implies both an inner connection and an outer connection with others and with all of creation. The truth of this crucial fact is essential for our lives, and it is confirmed in scientifically proven ways.

John Masefield writes that we are "…held in cohesion by unresting cells."

Our interconnectedness in creation is akin to the radio waves that are present everywhere and are available to everyone at any time, but undetectable and unnoticed until we tune in to them. The energy and the power of our connectedness are constantly on tap.

Longfellow wrote, "All your strength is in your union."

Everything is connected. First, the air we breathe together keeps us all alive. We are also connected by the way we choose to live our lives, for everything we think, do, or say has an effect on someone, somewhere. When we begin to realize this, on a deeper level we can see that it is our Creator that connects everything in life, from start to finish.

As connected and creative human beings endowed with energy and power, we are constantly rediscovering who we are. What we have forgotten is that our energy, power and essence are the same as that of our Creator. The energy we use daily in thought, word, and deed is available because of our connection to God's energy which manifests through us, both individually and communally.

The Commission on Children at risk (sponsored by the YMCA of the USA, Dartmouth Medical School and the Institute for American Values) recently issued a major report, *Hardwired to Connect,* in which it argues that the loss of connectedness is devastating America's youth. The Commissioners believe that human beings may also be hardwired for transcendent connections. Relationships within the community are the key to assisting our youth in developing into responsible, caring and balanced adults.

The good news is that we are free to join together with like souls everywhere to refashion a world of our own choosing, a world that is created in God's image. A world where, through our connectedness, we demonstrate God's love in action. A world where no actions we take will disempower others.

To effect change in our world, first we need to engender the feeling within us that it has already happened—not just physically but emotionally and spiritually as well. Quantum physics confirms that creation responds to such feelings when we are certain of the connection between our inner and outer worlds and live as if the change has taken place. The change may not be outwardly apparent at any given moment, but the feeling "as if" it has already happened will eventually bring about the desired manifestation.

William James said, "If you want a quality, act as if you already have it."

The September 11 attacks have provided ample evidence just how inter-connected our lives are. There has been a ripple effect from these tragic events over the entire world, both negative and positive. The shock rendered people speechless initially. Spoken words were inadequate, but the feeling of rapport and connection among those affected created a climate of kindness and generosity. Several books have now been written describing the unparalleled aid and comfort given the injured and grief stricken. The event of 9/11 has also fostered alliances that have led to growing numbers of interfaith gatherings and prayers all over the globe.

"Since the civilized world is now united by electronic bonds into one body in constant and instant communication, it is largely interdependent and rapidly becoming more so. No nation can go to war now against another nation without going to war against all humanity. The world has become a family." Andrew Carnegie, 1907

Arnold Toynbee said that, "We are in the first age since the dawn of civilization in which people have dared to think it practicable to make the benefits of civilization available to the whole human race."

As you walk or drive through your town or neighborhood, do you sense an energy of interconnectedness? Why, or why not?

Is there some way you can feel connected to the homeless person on the corner or with the faceless person across the ocean, in the same way you feel a connection with family and friends?

When was the last time you felt connected to someone or to some thing outside yourself? When was the last time you felt the presence of that ultimate of all connections in your life, your Creator? Is it possible for you to describe this experience? How connected are you feeling at this moment?

create

The word create is derived from the Latin, *creare* and *crescere*, meaning to cause to grow or to come into existence. We usually think of this word as conveying a conscious, positive, God-like action and energy, yet we also experience the effects of our own unconscious creative energy and that of others, sometimes in negative ways.

Ralph Waldo Emerson wrote, "A man is what he thinks about all day long," and Henry David Thoreau said that "Events, circumstances, etc. have their origin in ourselves. They spring from seeds which we have sown."

Many today see themselves as victims, not in control of their own destiny. Some feel that they are victims of a God who makes choices for them. There are those who view their lives as controlled by genes and circumstances of birth.

Our lives are formed by conceptions and misconceptions of who we are.

"The words 'I am' are potent words; be careful what you hitch them to. The thing you're claiming has a way of reaching back and claiming you." A.L. Kitzelman

What we experience in the present moment, right now, is the result of what we have created in the past. However, we can change the future. We can observe the emotions we are feeling and monitor the thoughts that allowed them to manifest. When critical thoughts come into our minds, the power of choice gives us the opportunity to transform them into a higher expression. The attitudes we create for ourselves reverberate out and affect all life around us.

In the words of Jose Ortega y Gasset, "Living is a constant process of deciding what we are going to do."

As long as we live in this world where everything is relative and filled with opposites and we see ourselves as a selfhood apart from God, we will continue to use our power of creation in unconscious ways. When we realize and implement the transformative power of love we can effectively build the bridges that will heal our differences.

"We must make the choices that enable us to fulfill the deepest capacities of our real selves." Thomas Merton

The freedom to use our creative powers as we choose is always at our command. It is awesome to recognize that our decisions already have and will in the future affect not only conditions and life on this planet but perhaps on other planets as well. The fact that we have advanced technology at our disposal today makes the consequences of the use of our power even more dramatic and dangerous than at any time in history.

As La Rochefoucauld said, "Nothing is impossible."

What kind of a world do you want to create? What kind of world are you creating within your own consciousness? How have you used your creative powers in the past? How does this affect your life today? How will you use this power in the future?

education

Education is derived from the Latin word *ducere*, meaning to lead or to draw out the talents. Education implies a method to encourage the flowering of each person's unique gifts or talents.

Taking a good look at the source of the word education can make us wonder if we have confused it with the word instruction which comes from *instruere*, meaning to build upon or build on to. Perhaps Yeats expressed it best when he said that, "Education is not the filling of a pail, but the lighting of a fire."

It is conceivable that the practice of packing information into us can in fact destroy our learning process. The 'packing' form of instruction, centering as it does mostly on the transmission of factual information, probably resulted from a theory of child training that is the converse of education in the truest and highest sense. This does not mean we do not need the information and tools of language, math, science, arts, etc., to develop our talents.

T.S. Eliot wrote that, "No one can become really educated without having pursued some study in which he took no interest. For it is a part of education to interest ourselves in subjects for which we have no aptitude."

Formal education may not even be the most profound source of learning for humans. The first lesson as infants and toddlers is to learn about the human form and how to navigate within its structure. We observe our parents and siblings for clues and begin to imitate their movements and interactions. From the moment we are born, we are in a constant mode of learning until the moment of our death. The study of near death experiences suggests that the learning process may even continue after our physical existence here is finished.

However, when we truly educate, according to the semantic root of the word, the informational tools and gifts of knowledge we have received can then be used appropriately and in harmony with the drawing out of our talents. Both are a means to an end, for a gifting to the world of the creative abilities that are within every person.

David Sarnoff, a pioneer in radio and television communication, said, "I believe that the true purpose of education is not only to fill man's mind with knowledge and his belly with food, but to deepen his spiritual insights."

The intuition involved in insight includes both the heart and mind and leads to a deep wisdom that goes beyond ordinary intelligence and knowledge.

"The intuitive mind is a sacred gift and the rational mind a faithful servant. We have created a society that honors the servant and has forgotten the gift." Albert Einstein

Reflect on your own education. Was there a fire lighted to explore and follow your heart's and mind's passion? Can you recall a time when your talents were drawn out, rather than information packed in? Who and what stirred your talent? Were you inspired to develop and use your unique gifts? Are you continuing to learn, to grow, and to express yourself?

enthusiasm

Enthusiasm is derived from the Greek *entheos*, meaning God-filled. It conveys a love of life.

Paul Scofield says, "Enthusiasm is life."

We usually think of enthusiasm as being excited about something or someone. Yet, the root of the word confirms that an earthly life of vitality and passion comes about from being what we call God-filled, or emanating from our Creator Source, the very breath of life itself.

The poet and mystic Kabir (1440-1518) wrote:

"Are you looking for me? I am in the next seat. My shoulder is against yours. You will not find me in stupas, not in Indian shrine rooms, nor in synagogues, not in cathedrals: not in masses, nor kirtans, not in legs winding around your own neck, nor in eating nothing but vegetables. When you really look for me, you will see me instantly—you will find me in the tiniest house of time. Kabir says: Student, tell me what is God? He is the breath inside the breath."

Since the higher aspirations and all the hopes of mankind have been centered for centuries in the word "God", it has become the most accepted word we have in the English language that refers to Deity.

"Enthusiasm signifies God in us." Madame de Stael

Have you ever followed your thoughts and recorded them for a day, observing where your enthusiasm really lies? Could this be where God is leading you?

When as a teenager Russ Leo heard the Mick Jagger song *I Can't get No Satisfaction*, he realized the drugs he was using to artificially bring himself enthusiasm were bringing instead dissatisfaction to his life. Hearing that song changed his whole life. He found where his strengths lay and began to use them to serve others.

There are always fresh opportunities to make creative use of our powerful Divine energy (enthusiasm), to become more aware of our deep inner truth, and to move in a direction that can bring the joy and fulfillment of our life's mission. Joseph Campbell says that such fulfillment and satisfaction comes from following one's bliss, or individual passion (enthusiasm).

"Enthusiasm is the greatest asset in the world. It beats money, power, and influence." Henry Chester

Can you recall an instance when you experienced the unbridled enthusiasm of childhood? Where were you and what were you doing at the time? Who were you with? What were your feelings? Are you aware of how your enthusiasm can bring great satisfaction into your life and the lives of others today?

fly

Fly is derived from the Medieval English *flien*, meaning to move above ground on wings, and from the Medieval English *flie*, meaning any flying insect. Fly also refers to all creatures of flight and what we have learned from them about movement above the ground, including the ability to soar like birds.

"The fly ought to be used as a symbol of impertinence and audacity, for whilst all other animals shun man more than anything else, and run away even before he comes near them, the fly lights upon his very nose." Arthur Schopenhauer

Is it possible that such audacious action of flies, which demonstrates so much confidence, may have challenged us to do what we thought we could never do—fly? It is interesting that so much of what we know about flight, or what is required to fly, is associated with that little insect.

"The problem [of flight] is too great for one man alone and unaided to solve in secret." Wilbur Wright, 1900

It is easy to appreciate the insects and creatures that we hold in wonderment, such as the butterfly, hatching from a cocoon and showing us that transformation is possible. The grace and beauty of birds in flight have inspired poets and artists for thousands of years. The hummingbird with its courage, strength, and perseverance, encourages us to follow its example. Who is not inspired at the spectacle of wild geese taking off in unison and soaring through the air so effortlessly in perfect formation?

"Lying under an acacia tree with the sound of the dawn around me, I realized more clearly the facts that man should never overlook: that the construction of an airplane, for instance, is simple when compared [with] a bird; that airplanes depend on an advanced civilization, and that where civilization is most advanced, few birds exist. I realized that if I had to choose, I would rather have birds than airplanes." Charles A. Lindbergh, in an interview shortly before his death, 1974

Just three years before the historic flight of their fixed wing powered aircraft on May 17, 1903 at Kitty Hawk, North Carolina, the Wright Brothers felt that it would take at least fifty more years to accomplish that feat. The world has seemed a lot smaller since that day.

"One can never consent to creep when one feels an impulse to soar." Helen Keller

George Jacques Danton wrote, "We must dare, and dare again, and go on daring."

What in your life challenges you to 'dare'? How do you feel about flying? Does it help to bring certain aspects of your life into perspective as you look down on the earth or up and out into the vast unknown universe?

freedom

Freedom is derived from the old Norse *frithr*, meaning love and peace. The soul of freedom thus tells us that it is an internal state of being.

How often do we think of freedom as having anything directly to do with the love and peace that have their origin within us? Usually we use the word freedom as if it is a state or a condition that comes about from circumstances or forces somewhere outside of us. Every day we can see where this line of thought leads.

The derivation of freedom shows that we are truly free only when we allow our activities and choices to be governed by love and peace. Franklin Delano Roosevelt's 'Four Freedoms' come to mind: freedom of expression, freedom of religion, freedom from want, and freedom from fear. He emphasized a social contract and the responsibility of society to guarantee these liberties. It follows, then, that true power and true freedom lie in enabling and supporting the individuality and sacredness of one another.

"The God who gave us life gave us liberty at the same time." Thomas Jefferson

We can feel the strength of freedom as we make our choices with the knowledge that on the soul level our freedom is unlimited and that we are powerful beings with God-given free will. The power that fills us is actually the love and peace of God. Freedom in this context is not only who we are, but also why we are here in the first place! It defines everything we do and bring to the world. We could view our lives as inconsequential, but the truth is that we all share in this unlimited potential of freedom. Thus, whenever we wonder how to make our lives creative and constructive, we can remember the power of our freedom and the meaning of its roots in love and peace.

"No one can rob us of our free will," and "No one is free who is not master of herself." Epictetus

One dramatic example of true freedom was the life of Viktor Frankl, a professor of psychiatry and neurology at the University of Vienna. He was imprisoned for three years at Auschwitz and other Nazi prisons where he endured incredible suffering and degradation. As a result, he developed a new psychotherapy and eventually wrote the book, *Man's Search For Meaning*. He describes how even prisoners in death camps have the opportunity for freedom to dwell in their hearts:

"We who lived in concentration camps can remember the men who walked through the huts comforting others, giving away their last piece of bread. They may have been few in number, but they offer sufficient proof that everything can be taken from a man but one thing: the last of the human freedoms—to choose one's attitude in any given set of circumstances, to choose one's own way....And there were always choices to make. Every day, every hour, offered the opportunity to make a decision, a decision which determined whether you would or would not submit to those powers which threatened to rob you of your very self, your inner freedom; which determined whether or not you would become the plaything of circumstances, renouncing freedom and dignity to become molded into the form of the typical inmate."

Others have found peace of mind in trying times. Nelson Mandela's endurance of his lengthy imprisonment is an outstanding example. He demonstrated how peace is tied not so much to one's exterior circumstances as it is to the interior state of being. The freedom of our souls is a given, and when we use this freedom to keep our minds at peace and maintain an inner stillness, our freedom cannot be taken away, regardless of what is occurring around us.

All great people have found the freedom of interior peace in some fashion. Some create art forms and some go to the woods, as did Henry David Thoreau who wrote in *On Walden Pond*, "I went to the woods because I wished to live deliberately, to front only the essential facts of life, and see if I could not learn what it had to teach, and not, when I came to die, discover that I had not lived."

You may recall the Beatle, George Harrison, who found the freedom of true peace by forgiving the person who stabbed and almost killed him. Another important example is Pope John Paul II, who kept his peace by going to visit his would-be assassin to forgive him. The Holy Father's loving heart demonstrated the freedom of his mind and tremendous spirit. If enough of us follow these and other like examples, we can eventually give back to the world the blessings that come from our free and peaceful hearts.

Poet George Moore wrote, "The difficulty in life is the choice."

Is there a more profound answer to the dilemma created by the concept of free will, or choice? Although we are free to make choices, the scope of our awareness either limits or enhances the quality and effectiveness of the decisions we are free to make and for which we are solely responsible.

Is it possible for you to align yourself with Divine Will to assist you in your daily choices and decision making?

human

Human is derived from the Latin *homo sapien*, the sage or wise aspect, and *humus*, meaning the earthborn animal part of us. The human is thus a being who is both humble and sagacious.

When we call ourselves human beings and not just humans, we imply that we measure our lives by far more than our mere physical existence or even our intellect. It is our understanding of what it means to "be" that distinguishes our consciousness from that of plants and animals. This self-awareness is a very unique gift from our Creator.

Until the 18th century, the words human and humane were interchangeable. This tells us that there was perhaps a time when charity and compassion and kindness were thought of as the hall-marks of human beings. Such hall-marks are characteristic of what we think of as the Divine within us or as our higher selves. How frequently do you equate 'human being' with 'humane person'? Although we often view humans as flawed or weak earthly beings, the derivation of this word makes the wise or Divine aspect of our nature very real.

Robert Lehman, President of the Fetzer Institute, is quoted in Dean Ornish's book *Love & Survival*, "If God is the source of life, and if God is love, then love creates life. All ancient traditions connect the spirit with healing through love."

Lehman describes all human relationships as spiritual. This goes back to the time of Martin Buber who wrote about the space between the 'I and Thou' as an actual spiritual entity. It is from this entity that we can be helped to become more conscious of the Divine or wise aspects of our being. Lehman adds that the movement now is that "...the unit of transformation is not the individual in isolation, as it has always been throughout history, but it's the individual in community, and the relationships which form the community."

"Man is at the bottom an animal, midway, a citizen, and at the top, divine. But the climate of this world is such that few ripen at the top." Henry Ward Beecher

Physician and author Dr. Brugh Joy, in describing the value of suffering as a doorway to transformation, says that experiencing a deep relationship, with all of its difficulties, can be transforming: "One begins to see the larger mystery play of life, that the whole thing is sacred."

This journey, with all of its traumas, failures, and successes, can actually motivate and empower us. Our story can, when we accept and live into its ups and downs, enable us to find hidden within it special gifts that are ours to give to the world. These experiences, which are uniquely ours, contain clues which are crucial in the discovery of and surrender to the Divine purpose for our being in this human dimension.

"There are many paths to wisdom, but each begins with a broken heart." Leonard Cohen

The next time you use the phrase "only human," consider the possibility that all of us are wise, spiritual beings that are having a humble human experience, as the root of this word conveys.

What qualities do you observe in yourself and others that demonstrate humaneness? Can you see what the lack of humaneness has caused in our world? How can you increase this quality in your life?

illusion

Illusion is derived from the Latin *illudere*, meaning to play against or to mock. We usually think of an illusion as the opposite of what we term real or reality. Yet illusion in some cultures is called *maya*, or earthly experience.

Webster's Dictionary states that "delusion, illusion, hallucination, mirage mean something which one accepts as true or real but which is actually false or unreal." According to Webster, illusion implies an ascription of truth or reality to that which only seems to be true or real.

"The center of every man's existence is a dream." G.K. Chesterton

In fact, many have intuited and written that the whole of this physical life is an illusion. This may be true; however, our experiences here are very real to us and we must 'be' here in order to learn and grow from them.

"Knowing others is wisdom, knowing yourself is Enlightenment." Lao-tzu

It is a constant struggle in a world of opposites like ours to decipher truth from fiction. We keep getting fooled or taken in by what seems to be real, when in actuality it isn't real or even the truth. When this happens to us, we feel mocked, betrayed, embarrassed, and inadequate. On the other hand, there are many times when we feel a great sense of gratitude and relief when our fears and judgments about a person or a frightening experience turn out to be just that —an illusion.

"We all live under the same sky, but we don't all have the same horizon." Konrad Adenauer

Finding the courage and the discernment to deal with our illusions is a constant challenge. When you accept that most of our experiences have an illusory aspect, we become less rigid and life becomes more enjoyable.

The main illusion that most of us have is that we are separate from our Creator. We have simply forgotten the connection to God that is indelible and that can never be severed, regardless of how hard we might try to break it or think we are estranged from it. It is this illusion, that we do not embody the absolute image of God, that leads to all the other illusions, which make life difficult for us.

"Is life so wretched? Isn't it rather your hands which are too small, your vision which is muddled? You are the one who must grow up." Dag Hammarskjold

What is your experience with illusions? Take a few minutes before going to sleep at night and as soon as you awaken in the morning to visualize: What do you want to achieve this day? What are specific ideas that can be accomplished? What kind of personality and character do you wish to embody? Declare in reality the positive news that is waiting in your heart. Do you find that this can come in many disguises?

isolation

Isolation is derived from the Latin words *solus* and *insula*, meaning to be separated, as an island. Isolation denotes a solitariness. In its popular usage, it can indicate being separated, but not necessarily by one's own choice.

"Seas but join the regions they divide." Alexander Pope

To be totally alone while living on this planet is hard to imagine. The fact is, when we choose some form of temporary isolation it may feel lonely and appear to us as separation, or it can be a time to renew one's spiritual and physical strength. Much emphasis is given today to our individuality and to the importance of maintaining time and space for one's self.

Some spiritual beliefs include the concept that our souls come to earth from a blissful place of peace, harmony and oneness. If this is true, birth into an individual physical form with our own special characteristics, traits and talents must be a shocking jolt to the soul. Perhaps our fear of isolation stems from an unconscious fear imprinted in our being during the birth process. When people lived in a tribal culture, isolation from the tribe was the ultimate punishment and usually resulted in death. Even in our modern world, teenagers go through much angst for fear of not being accepted by their peer group.

In the words of J. Montgomery, we are "distinct as the billows, yet one as the sea."

If we see ourselves as tiny separate drops in the ocean, we can feel powerless. Have we forgotten that without each drop fulfilling its purpose and joined together with other drops of water there would be no powerful sea?

"To think you are separate from God is to remain separate from your own being." D.M. Street

Feelings and concerns surrounding a sense of isolation are, and always have been, a major problem and challenge for humankind. Finding ways to address the problems caused by isolation place this challenge in the same ranking with the issues of freedom, meaning, and death.

"A human being is a part of the whole called the 'universe,' a part limited in time and space. He experiences himself, his thoughts and feelings, as something separated from the rest, a kind of optical delusion of…consciousness. This delusion is a kind of prison for us, restricting us to our personal desires and to affection for a few persons nearest to us. Our task must be to free ourselves from this prison by widening our circle of compassion to embrace all living creatures and the whole of nature in all its beauty. Nobody is able to achieve this completely, but the striving for such achievement is in itself part of the liberation and a foundation for inner security." Albert Einstein

Through constant criticism and unrealistic expectations of others, and of ourselves, we can create a wall of self-imposed isolation around us. The opposite is also true, because our thoughts can create a deeper love and appreciation for the uniqueness of others, and for ourselves. This can remove obstacles that might break a sense of community and bring about the feeling of isolation.

"Like the body that is made up of different limbs and organs, all mortal creatures exist depending upon one another." Hindu Proverb

We all share in common the gift and wonder of both individuality and of being alive, whether together or apart. We are told by the scientific community that we are connected with all and everything that exists in creation, regardless of how isolated our physical forms appear on earth. In addition, Luke 17:21 tells us that, "The kingdom of God is within you."

"There are no masters and there are no disciples. Everyone has the same capacities." James V. Goure

Does being alone make you feel isolated or fearful? On the other hand, can you see that having time to be alone is a gift? Can you choose to find time to be by yourself each day? If so, you may find this to be a source of strength that makes you feel more connected to others and possibly a time of self-discovery.

light

Light is derived from the Latin *lucere*, which means to shine, and also from the Greek *pyloros*, or body parts, often referred to as the temple. According to the soul of light, it shines inside our 'body temple' as well as in the world outside of us.

"God is Light. God is said to be absolute—and in physics so is light." Peter Russell

We are told by science that light consists of electromagnetic radiation that stimulates sight and makes things visible. John Wheeler, physicist and a colleague of Albert Einstein, said that according to the rules of quantum mechanics, our observations influence the universe at the most fundamental levels. He looked at the basic constituents of reality, atoms, and the particles of light called protons, and observed that what he saw depended on how he set up the experiment. Thus, there was an interactive effect. In addition, modern physics tells us that there is really no reality to darkness, it is merely the effect of the absence of light.

The physicist James Goure observed that all energy is light and that various types of energy radiate out from human beings. He declared that this light that we emit can improve the world around us through positive prayerful thoughts, feelings, and actions. In fact, Jesus told us in the Sermon on the Mount, "Ye are the light of the world." Matthew 5:14

"As the Light of the world, you are the source of Love for everything in and on planet Earth." James Goure

How many of us really accept this fact, that we are the light of the world? The scientific world agrees that we are light. It remains for us to find ways individually of fulfilling our responsibility of being the bearers of light in the world. To start, we can nurture with kindness those around us, recognize light within every person, and affirm the power of healing inherent in that light. Before we go into any kind of meeting, business or otherwise, or before speaking to someone on the phone, especially if difficulty or conflict might be involved, we can visualize them filled with light and ask inwardly that all hearts can be opened so that the highest good of all will be the result. As we expand our awareness and put this into actual practice, the whole planet can be effectively changed.

We often speak of light as deep knowledge or as that which bears truth. For instance, we say we want to be "enlightened." After such a statement, quiet guidance will respond as we listen deeply for both internal and external messages. The answer may come from a myriad of forms and sources, or it may come synchronistically from hearing pertinent information when you least expect it. Light is everywhere, in everyone and everything, even in the darkness where we cannot see!

It is thought that our visual capability allows us to see only a fraction of the amount of light that exists everywhere. As a result, we are often not aware that what we see as darkness carries light within it. If light fills us and surrounds us, and exists everywhere connecting everything, even what we perceive as darkness, then it follows that we are truly light beings in the best, highest, and most literal sense.

Have you ever thought of your body as a temple? Have you spent much time learning how to respect your body as a holy place of light? Do you see all physical forms as sacred vessels? Do you remember that the light within you helps to keep the light of others burning brightly in this world?

My family and I have a daily practice that helps us balance mind, body, and spirit. We call it "giving Light" to each other. Anyone can consciously convey this Light energy, which is universal Divine energy flowing through us to another person. The light that is transmitted raises the vibrations of the physical, mental, and spiritual bodies of both the giver and the receiver, thereby enabling each to live out their day in more enlightened, peaceful, powerful ways.

There are, of course, other ways of being Light to others that are equally meaningful and helpful. Just a brief and intentional sending of a loving thought to someone near or far, whatever their circumstances, can have a very beneficial effect. In Lowell's words, it can be "Medicinal as light."

New research documents a concrete use of unseen light as medicinal by the application of ultraviolet light. The pilot study found that this unseen light can heal what is known as 'sick building syndrome' by sterilizing air conditioning systems and eradicating harmful bacteria, mold and other microbes that have been known to make occupants of these buildings sick. It may also be potentially effective in fighting harmful airborne biological agents.

Remember, your light is necessary to keep the light of others burning brightly, just as you depend on their light to keep the lights of your temple aflame. We are inextricably united in light.

"Light is the universal oneness of everything." James Goure

What is your experience with the power of light? Are you aware that together, the intensity of our unified light, expressed as love, can light the fire that will transform the world?

love

Love is derived from the Old English, *leaf*, meaning to permit or cause and from the Sanskrit, *lubh*, meaning desire. Love is therefore equated with the cause of life.

We commonly think of love as benevolent feelings and use it as a term of endearment or to express affection. How often do you equate love with our "life force?" How often do you equate love with the freedom that the Creator of our life force gives us?

"Because love is who you are, you will never fully comprehend its mysteries. Because Love is who God is, love is the Divine Mystery. It cannot be defined." Glenda Green

"Love is the only power in life, and it is the original point to which all vectors of thought are connected. Where there are contradictory thoughts, there also will be difficulties. Until one's relationship to love is changed in the heart, nothing fundamental will change in life. What is perceived as negative emotion is not the absence of love, but merely reversals of thought which are undermining love's power and goodness. Love disabled by negative thoughts can be a dangerous thing, for there is no greater power than love, and nothing closer to the soul." Glenda Green

The energy of love can be compared to water, which on the one hand sustains and enhances life, and on the other hand can cause much harm.

"If I speak with the tongues of men and of angels, but have not love, I am become as sounding brass or a clanging gong..." I Corinthians 13:1

People search for love in many different ways. Often we look to another person to complete what we feel is lacking in ourselves. This is a primary cause for the breakdown in so many relationships. Either we do not know or we have forgotten that love is the essence within each of us. Overlooking this fact has generated the misunderstanding that our consciousness is somehow separated from our true nature, which is love. While everything else in life is constantly changing, only love—the essence of life itself—remains the enduring constant.

Mahatma Gandhi wrote:

"We must either let the Law of Love rule us through and through or not at all. Love among ourselves based on hatred of others breaks down under the slightest pressure. The fact is such love is never real love. It is an armed peace. And so it will be in this great movement in the West against war. War will only be stopped when the conscience of mankind has become sufficiently elevated to recognize the undisputed supremacy of the Law of Love in all the walks of life....Whether mankind will consciously follow the law of love I do not know. But that need not perturb us. The law will work, just as the law of gravitation will work whether we accept it or no. The person who discovered for us the law of love was a far greater scientist than any of our modern scientists. Only our explorations have not gone far enough and so it is not possible for everyone to see all its workings."

If the law of love ruled politics, religions, businesses, corporations, educational institutions, and all other aspects of life, what would our world look like? Would it revolutionize life on the planet?

Many of our human emotions seem to block love. Is it possible that people who are hurting and often hurting others simply are not able to show love, and have forgotten that their true nature is love? Instead of harshly judging others, can we discern that most interactions are either a sharing of love or a cry for love? Violence in all of its forms, under this spiritual law, would be a desperate cry for love and help.

"...perfect love casteth out fear." I John 4:18

We all find it difficult to love those who do not seem to love us. Can we have faith enough in the power of love to look beyond hateful actions to the seeds of love that are planted in every soul, regardless of how hidden they may be?

"Love alone is capable of uniting living beings in such a way as to complete and fulfill them, for it alone takes them and joins them by what is deepest in themselves." Pierre Teilhard de Chardin

Have you ever looked at love from this point of view expressed by the soul of this word? How does this expanded concept of love fit into your life from this point forward? How are you going to express this new understanding of love in your everyday life?

mind

Mind is derived from the Sanskrit, *manas*, meaning to think, and from the Latin *mens*, which in English became mental. Mind is thus the mental, or the aspect of our personal energy, that allows us to hold thoughts.

The soul of the word mind therefore refers to more than just our brain's capacity, as some believe. Mind is more than the physical brain. While it is an energy in the brain's activity, the mind's intentions can both consciously and unconsciously affect everyone and everything.

According to the physicist James V. Goure, "The brain is physical and remains with the physical body when it is left behind in what we call death. The mind cannot die; it is one with mind universally present everywhere and throughout all time...and beyond."

"The mind of man is capable of anything—because everything is in it, all the past as well as all the future." Joseph Conrad

The human mind is truly amazing in every sense. For example we can actually feel our bodies responding to thoughts beamed from the mind. We are beginning to learn more and more about how our bodies are emotionally connected to our minds.

"The body, like everything else in life, is a mirror of our inner thoughts and beliefs. The body is always talking to us. We just have to take the time to listen." Louise Hay

Our bodies and minds are also greatly influenced by our soul, the individualized expression of our Spirit. This is the nonlocal aspect of our beingness that emanates from the Absolute.

"I think that there are interpersonal, nonlocal consciousness-mediated events through which one individual can influence another individual's health." Dr. Larry Dossey

It is useful to be aware that the energy of mass or collective consciousness contains the sum totals of both positive and negative thought forms projected out all over the world. Everyone is powerfully influenced by these unseen forces for good or ill, and most of us are affected unknowingly.

"Minds were designed for carrying out the orders of the heart." Emmanuel

One of our mind's functions is to allow us to remember the past and project into the future. It is important to remember to focus our mind on the present, consciously still its voice, and allow our Divine presence to direct our thoughts and actions. In the Buddhist tradition there is a practice called 'mindfulness' that can stimulate confidence in ourselves by making us less prone to the habitual fears and self doubts that lie deep in our unconscious and often undermine our greatest aspirations. The effort is in the moment to be awake and aware of the freedom and wisdom available to us. This practice is also referred to as living "consciously."

"That mind and soul, according well, may make one music." Tennyson

Are you aware of the power of mass consciousness? Can you think of instances when it might have affected you? Do you just accept the impressions that you receive from the world around you without careful evaluation? Whenever negative thoughts become repetitive, do you silently observe them to determine if they are coming from within you or from an outside source? From now on can you use your mind to create a safe place for yourself from the center of love within you?

mystery

Mystery is derived from the Latin *mysterium*, meaning the Divine secret. We usually think of a mystery as a puzzle that needs to be solved. The soul of mystery, however, indicates something deeper stemming from Divine knowledge that is beyond human understanding and having to do with ultimate answers to existence.

"God hath not made a creature that can comprehend him...The created world is but a small parenthesis in eternity." T. Browne

Humans are still at work trying to unlock every secret and mystery of the universe. Theoretical astrophysicists struggle to understand clues to the origin of diversity in planetary systems. The 'New Physics' has been able to shed some light on the impenetrable mystery of existence that surrounds us and of which we are a part. Such investigations, with resulting discoveries, are spiritual revelations as well. One breakthrough was the discovery by Einstein of the Unified Field Theory. It tells us we, and all that exists, are created from the same energy, yet endlessly and mysteriously diversified and different. The essence of this theory is a fact both known and proclaimed by mythology and various philosophies and religions for thousands of years.

"That no one can make a definite statement about its [unified field theory's] confirmation or non-confirmation results from the fact that there are no methods of affirming anything with respect to solutions that do not yield to the peculiarities of such a complicated nonlinear system of equations. It is even possible that no one will ever know." Albert Einstein

Most now agree that since there is only one supreme and ultimate image in which we are all created, it follows that we cannot be separate either from God or from one another.

Physicist Fred Alan Wolfe in an interview with Ronald Miller said, "Quantum physics shows us that matter is how spirit appears in the physical universe."

"God is not an illusion, but a symbol pointing beyond itself to the realization of the mystery of at-one-ment." Joseph Campbell

Physicist Brian Greene in his book *The Elegant Universe*, investigates vibrating strands of energy called strings that are thought to contain all the fundamental particles of nature—everything in the universe. It is sometimes called 'the theory of everything.' Ed Whitten, physicist and mathematician, has been dubbed 'the new Einstein.' He and many others continue to explore the mystery and seek to master the rhythm of the strings. The string theory contemplates that there may be eleven parallel dimensions or universes and shows space to be more dynamic and changeable than Einstein considered possible.

"The fairest thing we can experience is the mysterious. It is the fundamental emotion which stands at the cradle of true art and true science. He who does not know it and can no longer wonder, no longer feel amazement, is as good as dead, a snuffed-out candle." Albert Einstein

The mysteries of physical creation are vast and unending. It is encouraging that scientists have recently found two resonant planets that seem to be 'humming in harmony.' It is my hope that this joyful model of harmony and unity in outer space can and will inspire us to develop loving, intelligent, harmonious, and cooperative attitudes and actions so that life on planet Earth can evolve in accordance with universal spiritual principles.

International author, teacher and healer Joel Goldsmith writes, "...our present life on earth is only an interval in eternity."

Have you ever pondered the true concept of mystery? Can you remember a mysterious experience that touched you deeply? When was it? Where did it happen? Were you able to let go and relax into the mystery with a sense of trust and peace?

mystical

Mystical is derived from the Latin *mysticus,* meaning something puzzling that happens to us in a way that can be awe inspiring. Mystical thus speaks of an experience in our everyday life that leads to a truth beyond our normal, human comprehension.

The soul of this word conveys the fact that we are able to experience the Divine within the ordinary course of life. This is different from the way we often think of mystical experience, as something that transports us out of reality or away from the world.

"God will be present, whether asked or not." Latin Proverb

Some of us are more aware than others of the mystical evolution of our souls. Andrew Harvey describes today's true mystic as a "revolutionary activist" who prays, meditates, and serves, but also votes and reads the newspaper.

"In loving the spiritual, you cannot despise the earthly." Joseph Campbell

There are people of every faith, or of no particular religious connection, who have what they call mystical experiences. When this occurs, they report feeling a strong and unified connection both with the Creator and with all of life. Some, like St. Paul, experience a blinding light. Others tell of inexplicable unifying experiences with nature. Their reality often becomes, like many through the ages, 'to be in the world, but not of it.'

As we explore the universe with ingenuity and dedication, we find a few answers having to do with mystical phenomena. However, to date, scientists have not been able to discover the origins of existence, even though Alan Guth's research at MIT on the 'inflation theory' (having to do with the constant expansion of the universe) attempts to describe the origin of some of the earth's matter. More recently, fifty-four collaborating international scientists announced finding signs of what they think is the last elusive building block of matter. In spite of this discovery, the final answers to existence are still beyond our human reason and understanding.

Could this explain why we, in varying degrees of consciousness and awareness, look to mystical experience to gain greater comprehension and direction? There are many experiences that some call miraculous which cannot be explained rationally, for instance when situations change as a result of prayer, focused thought, or in some cases even for no apparent reason.

"Breaking the ideals of society is the path of the mystic." Joseph Campbell

"God does not die when we cease to believe in a personal deity, but we die on the day when our lives cease to be illuminated by the steady radiance renewed daily of a wonder, the source of which is beyond all reason." Dag Hammarskjold

What kind of experiences have you had that you would consider mystical? Have you experienced a connection with a higher creative intelligence? If so, how has this affected your life?

peace

Peace is derived from the Latin *pax*, meaning the Goddess of Peace who oversees peaceful agreement between belligerents, and from the Latin *paction*, meaning to make a covenant. Peace stems from the feminine aspect of ourselves, which is inherent in both females and males. The soul of peace indicates that it is the feminine principal that facilitates peace.

All of us have the innate, intuitive ability to be peacemakers. First, we need to recognize and put into practice the feminine quality of peaceableness that is within each of us. This is an active force that we see many women and men put to good and effective use—for instance, in child rearing and in the sorting out of sibling and family disputes.

"Something feminine—not effeminate mind—is discoverable in the countenance of all men of genius." Samuel Coleridge

Joseph Campbell, among many others, has indicated that if we were to recognize and experience peace in our own lives, the world would naturally come to peaceful ways of being, one person at a time. He wrote, "Our job is to straighten out our own lives."

If we stay in touch with our feminine aspect, we will come to realize that it is the universal principle of Divine receptivity, a creative, intuitive force that moves us to take dynamic, energetic, relational, community-building initiatives. For instance, Robert Muller, former Assistant Secretary General of the U.N., continued his lifelong career as an emissary of peace by establishing Peace University in Costa Rica. Others have launched a movement to establish a federal government Cabinet-level Department of Peace. Broad public support is needed to make this happen. Physicist Dr. John Hagelin, an affiliate of the Institute of Science, Technology and Public Policy at Fairfield, Iowa, has inaugurated a Unified Field-Based University of Peace with branch campuses to be located world-wide. He has been researching how to access the fundamental, universal field of peace that lies deep within the consciousness of everyone.

"There is only one journey. Going inside yourself."
Rainer Maria Rilke

Can we activate the feminine aspect inherent within all of us that can help us stay in a peaceable place internally, regardless of what may be happening around us?

"She who is centered in the Tao can go where she wishes without danger. She perceives the universal harmony, even amid great pain, because she has found peace in her heart."
Tao Te Ching

"What leads to peace is not violence but peaceableness, which is not passivity, but an alert, informed, practiced, and active state of being....And here we have an inescapable duty to notice also that war is profitable, whereas the means of peaceableness being cheap or free, make no money."
Wendell Berry

"If we have no peace, it is because we have forgotten that we belong to each other." Mother Teresa

When was the last time you felt deeply in touch with your peaceful feminine side? What caused you to feel this way? In what way can this be an asset for you in the future?

perfection

Perfection is derived from the Latin *perficere*, meaning to make, to do thoroughly, or to be complete. Perfection thus connotes a wholeness.

We usually think of perfection as a state of being or as a situation that is beyond normal human reach or attainment. Perfection as a universal principle is difficult to comprehend within the realm of our human perspective. However, the soul of the word implies that wholeness to some degree is indeed possible.

There is a spark within us that excites us to strive for and to achieve the corollary of perfection, which is to be whole or complete. This is entirely different from the perfectionism that motivates us to strive for the impossible.

Malcolm Forbes, writing in jest, says, "If you're looking for perfection, look in the mirror. If you find it there, expect it elsewhere."

Some faith traditions set perfection as a goal of life. The exhortation, 'Be ye perfect,' without a broad interpretation could be viewed as a fearful and hard command, which could make us feel inadequate or certainly less than whole. However, if we are already part of the perfection of God in our essence, is there any reason to think that we lack or need anything?

"He censures God who quarrels with the imperfections of men." Burke

Many have been schooled in the philosophy of Descartes which fosters the concept of separation and causes a serious misunderstanding of who we are. This can lead us to conclude we must struggle to become 'perfect'. We continually forget that we share the perfect image of God, now and forever.

"Our self image, strongly held, essentially determines what we become." Maxwell Maltz

"Live as if you like yourself, and it may happen." Marge Piercy

How would it be if you saw every experience as perfect for your soul's evolution and growth, or acted 'as if' it were? What would happen if you acted 'as if' and, therefore, 'knew' that all of life's experiences and stages were bringing a perfect future? Would there then be anything to worry about? Would you be free to let go and enjoy life?

"If you want a quality, act as if you already had it." William James

How would your life be different if, instead of seeking what many think of as perfection, you accepted your wholeness? Can you accept and love your whole self, just as you are in this present moment? How does it make you feel if you accept everything that is happening to you and around you, and trust that there is a Divinely ordered, loving purpose?

play

Play is derived from the old English *plega* and from the Medieval Dutch *pleyen*, meaning to play, frolic, pay attention to, and from the Greek *pflegen*, meaning to be answerable for. Play refers to both recreation and to performance.

How often do you forget to pay attention to your need to have some 'playtime' in our very serious and production oriented society? So many pressures, demands, and concerns can stifle our ability to relax, to let go and play.

We associate the ability to play easily with cheerfulness and the ability to be light-hearted. Perhaps this 'lightening' of our lives is what brings us close to the joy of enlightenment!

Yet, we rarely think about what we are told from the soul of the word play; that we are answerable for both finding the time for play and for what we do with our playtime. This responsibility is also true for our performance in the drama that we compose and act out in our everyday lives.

"All the world's a stage, and all the men and women merely players." Shakespeare

As in so many areas of life, working toward a healthy and satisfying balance in the work/play area is tremendously important. Higher and better performance comes from a rested, healthy worker. The semantic root of play reminds us that we are the writers of our personal, individual play, or drama, as well as the actors and directors responsible for the performance. Achieving balance in both recreation and performance enhances our well being.

When was the last time you took time out to play? Who were you with? How can you create more times to bring balance to your work life in the future?

priest

Priest is derived from the Greek *presbys*, meaning old, and from the comparative form, *presbyterous*, meaning elder. Usually we think of a priest as an ordained minister or cleric, yet the soul of the word implies that an 'elder' may be anyone who has attained wisdom.

It is more important than ever that we rediscover the true meaning of priest, characterized by the possibility of true priestly wisdom, in ourselves and in others.

Walt Whitman dreamed of, "a religion in which every person shall be their own priest...through the divinity of themselves."

This derivation of priest can make us wonder if all older souls are not meant to lead or shepherd those who are younger into a higher consciousness and awareness of the divinity within everyone and everything.

"Priests are extremely like other men, and neither the better or worse for wearing a gown or a surplice." Chesterfield

We can be guided by our inner universal intelligence which can act as our priest or pastor. This voice can lead in many ways, even to give pastoral care to others.

The gifts of higher consciousness and wisdom shared with us by elder presbyters or priests can serve as our ordination and authorization to minister as priests to others. By our birth right are we all called to priesthood, in the original and fullest sense of the word? What would the working world be like if all CEOs of corporations, every board member, and all workers were to see their role as a 'ministry' to one another and the world? What if this became a reality everywhere with everyone?

Has there been a wise person who has helped to guide you in your life? If so, is this person ordained a priest? Did he or she help you become aware of your Divine essence, your own divinity? Do you find that at times you can in your own Divine right be a priest to yourself or to others? Are the attitudes and energies with which you approach and perform your work as important to you as the end result?

religion

Religion is derived from the Latin, *religio*, meaning a linking or binding back to one's spiritual Source. Therefore, religion is meant not only to keep us connected to our Source but to reconnect and restore us to it when we lose our way. This adds more depth to the meaning of the word than the way many may think of it—as merely an adherence to a particular set of beliefs, creeds and rituals.

Huston Smith, expert on the world's religions, suggests that all the wisdom that human beings have conceived can be found in all the world's great, enduring religions. Even though ample wisdom is found within religions, the wisdom can be hidden due to the literal translation and or misinterpretation of each tradition's sacred scriptures that were written for other cultures and times. Often when original belief systems are misinterpreted or distorted, they bring us the opposite of a reconnection to God and to one another.

Most religions are organized around the belief that everything and everyone is separate from the Source/Diety. However, if we explore carefully the soul of the word religion, true religion would link us back to that Source, the epitome of love, peace, joy, harmony and wisdom realized through the experience of a depth of connection with God and one another. Some religious and faith traditions have recognized this fact and are attempting to rectify this issue within the context of their communities.

Sharon Sallzberg describes the core of faith as "your own inherent capacity for wisdom and love."

"We measure all religions by their civilizing power." Ralph Waldo Emerson

"Man is made by his beliefs. As he believes, so he is." Bhagavad Gita

The meanings of words used for various religious expressions are highly complex and full of intricate twists and turns. In fact, adherents within most religions vary greatly, not only in their interpretations of doctrines, but also in the way they practice their faith. This has been true throughout history and continues today.

Just think of all the different words used for our common Source: Allah, Krishna, Vishnu, God, Yahweh, Jehovah, Elohim, Lord, Adonai, Hari, Rama, Great Spirit, and others! Is there a way for the established world religions to come together in a peace and unity that honors all of the unique wisdom and differences of each? Could this unification take place on a purely spiritual level that is on a higher plane and beyond the religions themselves?

"Mark Twain's religion was a faith too wide for doctrines —a benevolence too limitless for creeds. From the beginning he strove against oppression, sham, and evil in every form. He despised meanness; he resented...everything that savored of persecution or a curtailment of human liberties." Albert Bigelow Paine

As human beings we all long for and seek this nexus with our Source and with each other. Author Hans Kung speaks of the possibility of a global and intercultural grounding for religion through a shared ethos where every human is treated humanely and all humans treat others as they want to be treated.

"Your daily life is your temple and your religion." Kahil Gibran

Einstein argued that two things were needed to prevent a Third World War: first, for all existing religions to join in one union of absolute love; and second, the creation of a World Youth Parliament. With such a new spiritual focus and spirit of cooperation among the world's religions, would it be conceivable for the young people of the world to usher in a wise, tolerant, caring, peaceful era?

If you have an affiliation with a particular religion, has it been helpful in keeping you deeply connected to God and to others? If you are associated with such a group or community, in what way does your participation contribute, not only to yourself, but to the greater world? If you do not follow any particular religious tradition, in what way does the soul of the word increase your understanding of the way religion is meant to serve mankind and the world?

soul

S oul is derived from the Medieval English, *soule;* its ultimate origin is undetermined, but the word came to mean
to be alone, or one soul appearing as many. This meaning is
in contrast to the way we usually think of souls, as relating
to the inner being of individual persons.

It is revealing that the soul of the word soul is as mysterious as our human experience of its reality. It conveys a
mysterious sense of connection to God and others while at
the same time we experience a distinct, separate identity.

"If the soul could have known God without the world,
the world would never have been created." Meister Eckhart

Regardless of how different our individual pursuits and
endeavors are in life, we each uniquely experience what I
call Soularity, a word that came to me through inspiration.
Soularity describes for me the authentic dance of our souls
or the process each of us creates as we attempt to integrate
our Divine and human selves. It entails a way of living our
shared life on Earth, while being ultimately connected to
higher dimensions.

"Thou whose exterior semblance doth belie-thy soul's
immensity." William Wordsworth.

The integration of these two aspects of our soul, essence
and ego, universal and personal, Divine and human, is a
continuing process. It can be thought of as an ongoing
dance that has the possibility of moving us beyond the idea

fostered by many in the scientific/material field that would have us believe the material creation is separated from the Divine.

"To think you are separate from God is to remain separate from your own being." D.M. Street

Soul can be thought of as the connector that emphasizes the oneness of our origin in unity that binds us together. Perhaps, as we remember this dance of all souls, we can banish the illusion of separation from our one Source that is known by many names. There are numerous metaphors to describe the experience we share: love, energy, light, the life force, God, and so on. Many attempt to capture this concept in words or in art and music and while they bring us closer, it always seems to remain outside our reach.

"God is like a mirror. The mirror never changes, but everybody who looks at it sees something different." Rabbi Harold Kushner

Each of the many religions and spiritual traditions established by humans is overflowing with indispensable souls that are like threads of radiant color composing a gigantic and majestic tapestry.

Have you ever felt a strong connection with another soul? What was happening at the time and how did you feel about it? What practices in your life have brought you closer to your soul? Would you consider setting aside a quiet time, with the intention of contacting a deeper part of yourself?

PART THREE

HEALING

A mong many ancient cultures, the healer was one of the most revered and treasured members of the community. In the modern world, this is reflected in the fact that most families are extremely proud of their children who become health care professionals. Healing is a gift, a skill and an art, and when we are fortunate enough to be healed, the resulting joy and good feeling are some of the most intense emotions we can experience. But like the words communication or enlightenment, healing is a word that incorporates many different facets. Examine the list of words in this section. Fear is there and so is death, but they are surrounded by the words balance, forgiveness, gratitude, and most importantly by humor. The resulting blend of these words can be one of the deepest emotional experiences we will ever have. Beethoven suffered from a variety of illnesses and was deaf for most of his adult life. In spite of this handicap, one of his greatest compositions and last works was a string quartet with the subtitle "A holy song of thanks from one who is healed after a long illness." It is music that combines both yearning and pain and also overwhelming joy.

Of course, physical healing is not the only kind of healing we need, as it is contingent on and interwoven with spiritual and emotional healing, which are far more elusive than healing of the body alone. Many of us do not know where to turn when our souls or our psyches need healing. When the terrorist attacks occurred on 9/11, hospitals, medical professionals, and all first responders raced to prepare to treat the massive onslaught of casualties. Tragically, the personnel at the treatment centers sat waiting for the most part, for those caught in the collapsing towers of the World Trade Center were beyond the reach of medical help. Yet the continuing need for healing of our hearts, minds, and spirits remains even today, not only in those cities and areas that were struck, but also across the U.S. and the world. Where will we find the healing we need? Take a look at other words in this section such as evil, ego, force, suffering. How are these a part of the healing process? In seeking the answers to this question, the answers will not come easily.

balance

The word balance is derived from the Latin *bilancem*, meaning to have two plates or scales that, when balanced, are even. When we think of something that connotes what we call balance, the thought brings up a feeling of harmony and ease. It is associated with a healthy way of being, such as a balanced or holistic body, mind, and spirit.

Studies in physiology and psychology recognize the left and the right hemispheres of the brain. Carl Jung and others in the psychological and spiritual fields see these two hemispheres as the male and female components within each of us.

"What is most beautiful in virile men is something feminine; what is most beautiful in feminine women is something masculine." Susan Sontag

Theodor Reik said that, "In our civilization, men are afraid that they will not be men enough and women are afraid that they might be considered only women."

If you feel out of harmony with the opposite sex, look at the masculine qualities of objectivity and reason connected to the energies of our minds, and at the feminine qualities of relationship and the gifts of intuition and feelings that stem from our emotions, to see if they need to be balanced. We must become consciously informed of the necessity for this dual soul integration in order to lead a creative, balanced life.

"If men and women are to understand each other, to enter into each other's nature with mutual sympathy, and to become capable of genuine comradeship, the foundation must be laid in youth." Havelock Ellis

The play of consciousness between the masculine and feminine principals of the universe is always seeking balance. This dance of energies is the very source of creation itself and is reflected in the natural world and in every aspect of human life on Earth. We are an integral part of the natural world and have the ability to heal our minds, emotions and bodies when we activate the intrinsic power of our spirits to affect this healthy balance. It is even possible to prevent all kinds of diseases and rejuvenate our bodies and minds at the cellular level. Balanced thought patterns can lead to new behavior that can stimulate a way of living that is more loving, stable, respectful and equal, or in a word, "balanced."

Look back in your early life to a time when you were first aware of a feeling of balance; what was happening around you? Who were you with? What comes to you as you move through thoughts of other times in your life when you felt out of balance? What did it feel like? Can you describe what was going on inside of you? Did it have to do with what we think of as masculine or feminine qualities? How did this affect your relationship with the opposite sex?

die/death

Die/death is derived from the old Norse *deyja* and the old English *dye*. The origin is unknown, but it was customary to use 'dye' to color cloth in order to make a living. The inference is that die refers to a way to continue to live, rather than our usual reference to the end of life.

The fact that the etymology of die and death is unknown reminds us again that our human experience of life, in its totality, is equally mysterious.

Robert Frost said that one reason for being on earth is to learn one principal thing about life, that it goes on.

Even though our loved ones may no longer be with us in physical form, we do not lose our memories of them or the continuing energy of their love and influence. I feel that this is their 'true essence' which remains with us. There is a Jewish saying that the only truly dead are the forgotten.

The poet Cid Cannan says "there is no meaning to the word *life* unless there is death."

Harriet Doerr, the novelist, describes the interval between birth and death as "scarcely more than a breathing space." Every second of life also carries death within it. At the moment of our birth, the process of death commences. The converse may also be true. Unless we let each moment of the past die, we cannot live in the present.

As I die to old experiences in life, I find that I live into new opportunities. Such dying does not often happen without pain, sorrow, and difficulty. No one is immune from these universal and sometimes traumatic events. There are lessons about this process that nature models for us. Not long after a forest has been burned over by fire, the life of the area begins again with the return of new growth and animal life. The resurgence of life comes to the dead area following a period of 'quiet' that is similar to winter.

"In nature there is less death and destruction than death and transmutation." Edwin Way Teale

Many books have been written about the near death experience (NDE), including the groundbreaking book by Dr. Raymond Moody *Life after Life*. Reports and details about these experiences vary, but there is a common theme of the enfoldment and infusion of a Divine love so profound that is is difficult to find words adequate to describe or share the experience. The vast majority tell of major changes in their lives which include a renewed enthusiasm for life, intense interest in the welfare of others, being led to a career change, a heightened compassion, and a complete lack of fear of dying and death. Such was the experience of author Dannion Brinkley, who prior to his NDE describes himself as a man who was selfish and unaware.

Some skeptics question the authenticity and validity of NDEs, claiming that these experiences are manifestations of the imagination or are brain induced hallucinations. However we choose to view NDEs, there is no doubt that they have had an extraordinary and permanent affect on people. It follows that the way we view and understand the inevitable end of life in physical form definitely influences the way we live our lives and how we relate to others.

Have you ever been in the presence of a person who is in the process of dying and noticed how they seem to want 'quietness' in their space?

"The water in a vessel is sparkling; the water in the sea is dark. The small truth has words that are clear; the great truth has great silence." Rabindranath Tagore

"Oh, but what can we take along
into that other realm? Not the art of looking,
which is learned so slowly, and nothing that
happened here. Nothing.
The sufferings, then. And above all, the heaviness,
and the long experience of love—just what is
wholly unsayable."

Ninth Duino Elegy, Rainer Maria Rilke,
translated by Stephen Mitchell

What has been your experience with loss and grief resulting from the death of others? Is the mystery at the root of the words die/death and the knowledge of its 'hopeful' usage of some comfort to you? Are you aware of all the experiences or moments in life that you have already had to die to? What new opportunities have come to you as a result? Has there been a growth or a renewal involved? What helps you to 'carry on' as you grieve for your losses?

ego

E go is a Latin word, related to the old English, *ic*, meaning I. Ego focuses on self-awareness or esteem and also on a devotion to one's own separate self, interests and feelings.

Shakespeare asks the central question, "Who is it that can tell me who I am?"

Often it seems that we understand the universe, which is not easy to comprehend, better than we understand our own egos.

In the words of G. K. Chesterton, "One may understand the cosmos, but never the ego; the self is more distant than any stars."

We frequently think of ego in a negative way or give egoism a negative connotation; however, a balanced ego is essential to our self-respect, self-realization, and esteem to be the unique self-aware persons that the root of this word suggests. An ego that is balanced is one that assists us to live and maintain our being in a world of opposites.

The ego is the part of us that truly experiences the separations and divisions of the world we see all around us. This part of us is a very important, positive force as long as it does not play the dominant role or assert authority over our spirit. Our ego is a necessary tool we use for navigating within this world. Without constant vigilance, however, the ego can dominate our lives and become both a stumbling block and a real obstacle to healthy relationships. The dictates of our ego can be recognized easily in any situation when we insist on being 'right' even when the facts do not support our opinion.

A Hindu proverb says, "There is nothing noble about being superior to some other person. The true nobility is in being superior to your previous self."

We each have a unique and authentic dance that takes place between our Divine source and our human expression. When we practice being the detached observer of our thoughts, feelings and emotions, we can prevent regrettable words and actions from polluting our lives. The moment we become aware that the ego has taken charge, it is possible through a shift in consciousness to allow a higher aspect of ourselves to be our guide. The positive results of this practice can be astounding.

We first need to let go of the egoic wars in our own minds and empower a place of peace there, which is a prerequisite for establishing peace in our world. Our ego can then merge with our authentic power of love and compassion and radiate in all that we think, say and do.

How do you live within the paradox of your ego and your Creator essence? Are you aware of the times when your ego is in control of your thoughts, feeling and emotions? How does it feel? What happens as a result? What do you experience when you allow the Divine within you to guide your decisions and actions?

evil

Evil is derived from the old English *yfel* and kin to the old English *ofer* and *up*, meaning over and up, or the basic idea of transgressing. Evil thus implies a movement to a place where one ought not to be.

When something appears to us to be evil, we need to consider that the mere belief either in a self or a condition that is separate from God may be the only real evil there is. Could it be that such a belief might lead to evil acts or to ill health?

Is a feeling of powerlessness involved when we feel separated from God, and can this need to feel powerfully in control lead to destructive actions?

"Where love rules there is no will to power and where power predominates love is lacking. The one is the shadow of the other." Carl Jung

Indeed, at many points and occasions in life we ask how we who are created in God's image could possibly speak and act as we do? Jeffrey Russell, author of *The Prince of Darkness: Radical Evil and the Power of Good in History*, says that we can recognize evil and "if we have any self-awareness, when we get angry, we recognize the evil impulse in ourselves."

Carl Jung says that there is a part of our humanity that is often denied, feared, or repressed, which he calls our shadow side. He goes on to argue that this shadow side of us needs to be embraced in order for us to be healed or made whole.

A destructive climate of evil, together with accompanying evil deeds that some label insane, stands in opposition to our experience of compassion and love. When this happens, transgression takes place and we choose to go where we are not supposed to be. Are we simply unaware that we can never separate ourselves from the love that is God's image?

If we accept that we are given the power of life in the image of God, through love itself, we recognize that our life essence is that Divine love. It follows that we are meant to express and manifest that love in order to have the kind of life we were destined to have. We can become alienated from this love or pervert its energy in inappropriate ways that we refer to as evil. When this happens, we are experiencing live spelled backward (evil), the opposite of the way we are meant to live. For instance some people think they are loving but place conditions on their love, or attempt to get something back that they think they need.

Erich Fromm wrote that immature love says, " I love you because I need you," but mature love says, "I need you because I love you."

In our freedom we have distorted our basic, beautiful life energy, our love, in many ways. In an attempt to avoid responsibility for our action, mankind has universally created a personified spirit of evil.

As comedian Flip Wilson used to say in jest, "The devil made me do it!"

There is no doubt that there are negative forces that can influence us to do negative things, however we are ultimately responsible for our choices. When we see ourselves as separate from others and when we separate ourselves from our actions, we experience the opposite of what being alive means, leading to various forms of destructive behavior. Some call this turning away from life "sin." We become vulnerable to what we term evil forces. The results of this can be observed by reading any newspaper.

Are you conscious of the fact that the love of God is with you in every moment you live? When you have committed yourself to a certain standard of behavior, have you ever experienced a confrontation with its opposite or what some call your shadow side? Have you been able to embrace this shadow side of yourself? Have you become more accepting of yourself and others as a result?

fear

Fear is derived from the old English *faer*, meaning danger or apprehension. It can convey trepidation, intimidation, or awe often resulting in anxiety and a lack of confidence.

The common connotation of fear is that it is a response to something outside of us that is frightening. However, according to The Foundation For Inner Peace, publisher of *A Course In Miracles*, there are only two basic emotions, love and fear, and the source of each emanates from within us. "Only your mind can produce fear."

Dr. Elizabeth Kubler Ross says that we are born with two instinctual fears, the fear of falling and the fear of loud noises, both of which come from a love within that wants us to survive in this earthly life. All other fears are learned.

"Just as courage imperils life, fear protects it." Leonardo da Vinci

"Fear is an emotion indispensable for survival." Hannah Arendt

Fears that are learned and internalized are sometimes known as 'false evidence appearing real,' or the acronym f-e-a-r. One of the most common learned fears is our resistance to and apprehension of change. Such fear is a response to challenges to our status quo and possible new directions for our life. This learned fear can limit us and block the courage that can lead us to follow our hearts and recognize our real passions in life. In other words, such a blockage to our courage stifles our ability to be true to ourselves.

Alan Paton wrote, "When men are ruled by fear, they strive to protect the very changes that will abate it."

"You gain strength, courage, and confidence by every experience in which you really stop to look fear in the face…You must do the thing you think you cannot do." Eleanor Roosevelt

"Fear is only an illusion. It is the illusion that creates the feeling of separateness—the false sense of isolation that exists only in your imagination." Jeraldine Saunders

We sometimes fear saying no because we fear rejection. Thus, we allow ourselves to be coerced into doing something we really don't wish to do. This fear is usually fostered by a lack of trust in our own integrity. I have had to learn over and over again that I am free to choose how to respond at all times and in every aspect of life, and do not have to be fearful or relinquish this authority and power to any form of intimidation or coercion. When we are aware that we always have a choice, then we can surrender any vestiges of victimhood that may have surfaced.

"It is better to have a right destroyed than to abandon it because of fear." Phillip Mann

David Spangler writes that the universal problem of fear in the world is not the fault of any one country or group. He understands it to be an ancient force, like a virus, "that moves openly in the world on feet of violence and suffering born of our failure to imagine the power of love."

"Neither a man nor a crowd nor a nation can be trusted to act humanely or to think sanely under the influence of a great fear." Bertrand Russell

President Franklin Delano Roosevelt will always be remembered for the following words that brought courage and hope to our nation, paralyzed with fear, in one of its darkest hours:

> "The only thing we have to fear is fear itself—nameless, unreasoning, unjustified terror which paralyzes needed efforts to convert retreat into advance."

Is it possible that when faced with fearful situations we could ask the question—'What would be the most loving response?' How would our world change if everyone responded on the basis of love? Would peoples and countries begin to share and talk out their fears; speak their truth; communicate their different views of the world, together with their dreams and hopes? What would be the result of such peaceful and peace-making dialogues? Do our creative responses to fear begin first in our own hearts and lives?

How do you sort out your helpful fears from the ones that block your progress? Think back to a time when fear prevented you from accepting a change or a challenge in your life. What did you miss by giving in to those feelings of fear? Was there a lack of confidence involved? What connects you to the ability to act in the face of your fears?

food

The word food is derived from the old English words *fodder*, which becomes feed, and *foster*, meaning to nourish or to nurture.

We are well aware that from the moment we arrive on earth and begin to use our physical bodies we are dependent on the nutrients in food to nourish our bodies. We often take this necessity for granted. Yet, most are unaware that the soul of this word indicates how importantly food nurtures our spirits as well as our bodies.

"More die in the United States from too much food than of too little." J.K. Galbraith.

Conscious, healthy eating is a loving way to nurture ourselves.

We have heard it said that we are what we eat. Yet, do we pay enough attention to where our food comes from or to the way it is grown? Do you ever give thought to those who grow it and who transport it to the market? For food to be truly nurturing, as the root of the word implies, important factors are the way it is prepared and served, together with the attitude of the handlers and servers. Thus, what a person puts into the presentation of the food is just as important as the consumption.

"A smiling face is half the meal." Latvian Proverb
Wendell Berry writes:

"Starting with the economies of food and farming, we should promote at home, and encourage the world abroad, the ideal of local self-sufficiency. We should recognize that this is the surest, the safest, and the cheapest way for the world to live. We should not countenance the loss or destruction of any local capacity to produce necessary goods."

There are many articles published today about which diets will maintain optimum nutrition for health and well being. Our food is a tangible blessing of energy along with the other building blocks of life, such as clean water and air. It requires education and motivation for it to be used in a balanced, life-giving, supportive way, one that can prevent many forms of illness—of body, of mind, and of spirit. Once we begin such 'mindfulness' concerning food, we can then start listening to our bodies to discern intuitively what they need to be fueled and nurtured appropriately. Beyond that, our hope is to find ways we can help one another to be fed (nurtured) in both body and soul.

While some raise concerns about what foods are healthy, safe, and delectable, thousands of others in our world who live in poverty and famine cry out for food aid to prevent starvation. For instance, a recent article in a Johannesburg newspaper stated there is a food crisis in six Southern African countries and that famine there threatens 14 million people! At the same time, the UN World Food Program estimates that just one percent of the food stockpiled in the wealthy, developed countries could remedy the hunger gap the world over.

"To a man with an empty stomach, food is God." Ghandi

We normally think of food as necessary to satisfy our hunger and keep us alive, yet some people have desperate hungers for nourishment other than food. For instance, those who are anorexic are obsessed with their body image and accompanying need for acceptance. In their frantic attempt to achieve this image, they abhor food to an extreme and become in grave danger of starvation. This condition only exists in countries that are materially affluent and is a testament to the fact that love, acceptance and nurturing are the most essential needs of humanity.

"I have the audacity to believe that people everywhere can have three meals a day for their bodies, education and culture for their minds, and dignity, equality, and freedom for their spirits. I believe that what self-centered men have torn down, men other-centered can build up." Dr. Martin Luther King

How are you affected when you contemplate that there are many people who do not have adequate food and on the other hand, others who starve themselves in the midst of plenty? Do you ever find yourself taking our abundant food supply for granted? Are you aware that it is the Love within the food, from production to consumption, that nourishes and nurtures you the most?

force

F orce is derived from the Latin *fortia*, meaning strength and comfort. Force is with us from birth and is what makes us strong or alive, also comfortable.

We often hear the quote from the movies, "May the force be with you." However, the soul of this word makes it clear that 'force' is already with us and that we are not separate from its strength and comfort. The fact is that what we call 'God' is the force of our bodies, minds, and spirits, otherwise there is no strength, comfort, life force, or existence. In the Christian Bible, the Holy Spirit is spoken of as the Holy Comforter, or as the presence of God sent to comfort and guide us.

The proper use of this life force or how we choose to use this force determines the results of our actions.

Martin Luther King, Jr., wrote, "Darkness cannot drive out darkness; only Light can do that. Hate cannot drive out hate; only love can do that. Hate multiplies hate, violence multiplies violence, toughness multiplies toughness in a descending spiral of destruction. The chain reaction of evil—hate begetting hate, wars producing more wars—must be broken, or we shall be plunged into the darkness of annihilation."

The Buddhist teacher Joseph Goldstein asks if we can see how the force for good or harm that we see in our world may in some way be in our minds and lives as well?

Anne O'Hara McCormick writes concerning force as power, "Today the real test of power is not the capacity to make war, but the capacity to prevent it."

"Wars are not fought for territory, but for words. Man's deadliest weapon is language. He is susceptible to being hypnotized by slogans as he is to infectious diseases. And where there is an epidemic, the group-mind takes over." Arthur Koestler

Reinhold Niebuhr said that even though violence breeds violence, pacifism and neutrality can allow violence to flourish, and when the use of violence to save lives is deemed necessary, the key is the ability not to harbor violence in one's heart. This is a confusing contradiction since we know from history and words spoken by all prior sages that problems are never solved by using the same means that caused them in the first place.

The Buddha himself spoke to the masses regarding the appropriateness of self-defense. Is it possible to act with wise and compassionate motives rather than with animosity and revenge? These are ongoing questions that have plagued human history.

What would our world be like if in a reformed and true unity of nations we lived by what Don Kraus and Mark Epstein call "the force of law rather than the law of force"?

When we think force is called for, perhaps we can remember that all life forces are joined, and visualize what the world would be like if we used this combined force to maintain a peaceful presence and be a comfort to one another.

Does the world need to develop more of what Buckminster Fuller called "livingry instead of weaponry"? He wrote, "Either war is obsolete or men are."

Are you aware of the considerable strength you experience from someone when they comfort you in a distressing moment? It also takes effort, a force from within you, to comfort others. Do you feel or sense how your inner strength is magnified when you give comfort? Has your expression of comfort brought life-giving strength, peace, and solace in return? Are you aware of the constant strength and comfort that your God-force offers you?

forgiveness

Forgiveness is derived from *give* and *gift*, which are derived from the old English *gifan* and the old Irish *gobim*, meaning to give and to take, respectively. The soul of forgiveness thus conveys both the giving and the receiving of gifts.

"Forgiveness is the giving, and so the receiving of life." George MacDonald

How often do we see opportunities for forgiveness as the simultaneous giving and receiving of a gift? In fact, to understand and then effectively apply acts of forgiveness in one's life is ultimately an act of love. Reinhold Niebuhr reinforces this fact with his words, "Forgiveness is the final form of love."

When was the last time you accepted a gift of forgiveness for yourself? If we are unable to accept and love ourselves we simply cannot receive this life-giving, all-important gift.

Even deep, heartfelt forgiveness is often a slow and continuing process through which both the giving and receiving of its gifts seep into our awareness and free our hearts and minds.

"To understand everything is to pardon everything." Madame de Stael

Recall a time when you felt resentment or wanted to blame another person, or a group, for something that caused you distress, pain, or unhappiness. Can you also remember a time when you chose to release the feeling of being the victim in such a painful situation and decided to take responsibility for the experience, even when it may have seemed to be another's fault? Did you feel you yourself received a gift from making that choice?

"Forgiveness is the way to true health and happiness." Gerald Jampolsky

The importance of the gifts of forgiveness is recognized as all-pervasive. Fred Suskin of Stanford University is teaching a continuing education course entitled *The Art and Science of Forgiveness*. In the course, Suskin shows his students how to view painful past experiences in ways that help them see themselves as survivors, not victims. Also, attorneys such as Karla Garret are using this forgiveness principle to effect win-win law practices. In the book *Radical Forgiveness* by Colin Tipping, principles of radical forgiveness are suggested that can be used as a tool for helping move either individuals or groups out of "victim consciousness."

Norman Cousins said that, "Life is an adventure in forgiveness."

We can conclude then that forgiveness is a gift of personal peace that we give to ourselves and to others.

"Forgiveness is all-powerful. Forgiveness heals all ills"; "The forgiving state of mind is a magnetic power for attracting good." Catherine Ponder

Can you see how you are responsible for your perception of any given experience? Have you noticed how your perceptions of past events can change over time?

When there is a giving and receiving of the gift of forgiveness, what do you imagine is happening? Can you feel the opening of your heart as you release emotions you have been carrying? Are there sorrows and regrets due to the pain you may have caused others or they may have caused you? Can you imagine the lightness in your heart when you have truly forgiven yourself?

gratitude

Gratitude is derived from the same root as the word *grace* or the Latin words *gratus*, meaning graciously or agreeable, and *gratulari*, meaning to render freely, to give thanks. The soul of gratitude refers to an attitude of heart and mind in which one finds life filled with gifts of grace freely received.

Thousands of words have been written on the important subject of gratitude. Meaningful and well-remembered words from the Bible on the subject of gratitude are, "In everything give thanks: for this is the will of God..." 2 Thessalonians 5:18

Have you ever tried to spend a day filled only with thoughts of gratitude, morning to night? Those who have tried this tell me that as a result, their hearts felt unburdened and they began to realize how all of their complaints or complaining had done nothing to change their situations or to enhance the quality of their lives. Instead, they reported that on their 'gratitude day' many unexpected things for which to be even more grateful seemed to multiply. How do you think our world would change if everyone filled their day with thoughts of gratitude alone?

In addition, our sincere expression of gratitude to others enables us to reach out to them with a love that touches their lives in healing and restoring ways. Have you noticed in your life what the root of the word gratitude implies? Are

136

there gifts of grace that come your way as you feel and express gratitude? As a result, do even more opportunities seem to happen that engender further gratitude? This wisdom is noted in all the great spiritual traditions.

"Thanksgiving for a former doth invite God to bestow a second benefit." Robert Herrick

When life presents us with painful experiences it may seem impossible to feel thankful. This is especially true on those occasions when it is difficult to recognize and accept responsibility for the part we may have played in bringing about any particular situation. The next time you feel the need to blame others, recall moments in your life when you felt guilty or unworthy, yet received acceptance and love from someone. Was the grace of gratitude involved?

New research conducted by Robert A. Emmons at the University of California at Davis and Michael E. McCullough of the University of Miami, published in the *Journal of Personality and Social Psychology*, shows that people who consciously remind themselves every day of the things they are grateful for show marked improvements in mental health and some aspects of physical health. The results appear to be equally true for healthy college students and people with incurable diseases.

"I find that it is not the circumstances in which we are placed, but the spirit in which we face them, that constitutes our comfort." Elizabeth T. King

Through the ages, sensitive souls have discovered that happiness is a chosen state of mind that is not necessarily connected with life circumstances and therefore goes hand in hand with gratitude.

"Everything has its wonders, even darkness and silence, and I learn whatever state I may be in, therein to be content." Helen Keller

In looking back, can you recall a difficult situation in which you can find a hidden gift? Can you feel some gratitude in spite of the circumstances? Observe your progress in areas of life where gratitude for certain happenings and perceptions is still hard to feel. As you search these experiences in a deeper way what insights can you be grateful for?

health

Health is derived from the Medieval *hole* and the old English *hal*, meaning sound or complete wholeness. Thus, to be healthy means that every part of our life is working together as a whole.

"Health is the thing that makes you feel that now is the best time of the year." Franklin Pierce Adams

We commonly think of health as the absence of disease. The soul of the word, however, illustrates that the true meaning of health has more to do with our complete or entire selves, mind, body, and spirit, operating together in a complementary, balanced, and harmonious fashion.

"Since the human body tends to move in the direction of its expectations—plus or minus—it is important to know that attitudes of confidence and determination are no less a part of the treatment program than medical science and technology." Norman Cousins

Holy and heal, two words related to health, help us discover where the holistic movement toward a healthy life originated. This approach to health care means taking into account the whole person, mind, body, and spirit, rather than treating the symptoms of a disease, or managing its effects only. It also encourages us to regard the whole of our lives on this planet and beyond as a sacred unity.

"You can promote your healing by your thinking." James E. Sweeny

There is a revival of this ancient knowledge and under-standing today as witnessed by the large numbers of persons now seeking the help of those doctors and others who offer the holistic approach to health. More and more people are making use of various healing modalities that are focused on the mind and spirit, as well as the physical body.

"The body manifests what the mind harbors." Jerry Augustine

Most of us know that our bodies are an interconnected whole with every part working together harmoniously when in a true state of health. It may be beyond our ability to imagine or fully comprehend, however, that each of us is an integral part of a greater whole. We only have to look at the diversity of our families, communities, nations, or our environment to see the great need for a healthy balance among our different races, in our justice systems, in our political systems, and in the business world, to name a few examples.

"The sorrow which has no vent in tears may make other organs weep." Henry Maudsley.

Jesus told us in John 14:12 that we have the power to do even greater works than he! How many of us really believe his words or try to put them into practice? Those who have discovered this inner power are enabled to live and to be on a level where the material and spiritual come together as a dynamic whole. They are able to ask for healing from the Creator and then pass it on to others to assist with the dif-ficulties and problems of everyday life that are common to all. This insight can be applied to family disagreements, the work place, and even in international challenges. Such heal-ing often happens in subtle ways, but there are times when it appears in miraculous ways. Have we forgotten the unlimited Creator aspect of our being that is beyond the parameters that circumscribe what we think of as the relative, physical world?

Are you aware of your power to help yourself and others heal? What are you now doing or could you do to bring that about? How can attaining greater health serve to enrich your life? How do you contribute to the health of the world around you?

humor

Humor is derived from the Latin word *complectere,* meaning to weave characteristics of a person, such as hot-cold, dry-moist—the four Humors. The meaning of humor has gone through three cycles of evolution. First, it described the four different aspects of our selves. In its second phase, it depicted a person as being in a good or bad humor or mood. Now, it has become a description of something that makes us laugh.

"Humor is the contemplation of the finite from the point of view of the infinite." Christian Morgenstern

It was not until the late 17th century that humor evolved to the modern meaning of funny.

The root of the word humor illustrates the way humor interlaces the funny with the serious. A person of good humor is enjoyable to be around, and they would never say or do anything that would be hurtful, downgrading, or damaging to another.

"Comedy is simply a funny way of being serious." Peter Ustinov

An Italian proverb says that "he who jokes confesses." Humor has been called the mark of our humanity.

"The ability to laugh at life is right at the top, with love and communication, in the hierarchy of our needs. Humor has much to do with pain; it exaggerates the anxieties and absurdities we feel, so that we gain distance and through laughter, relief." Sara Davidson

The implication is that humor often comes about after time passes and one looks back on a chaotic, emotional experience which, in retrospect, appears humorous. It is essential to be aware of when we might be using humor to trivialize and escape from important issues that may be confronting us or to use it to mask our true feelings.

"Humor is emotional chaos remembered in tranquility." James Thurber

"Laughter is the closest thing to the grace of God." Karl Barth

Good humor can reflect a humble and kind state of mind and heart, also a positive, uplifting outlook on life.

"Humor is an affirmation of dignity, a declaration of man's superiority to all that befalls him." Romain Gray

How has humor given you perspective in your life? When life presents challenges, can you search for the humor that could bring a sense of ease and balance?

paradox

The word paradox is derived from the Greek words *dokein*, dogma, *doxa*, to believe, *orthodoxos*, right or true opinion, and from *paradoxos*, contrary to or beyond right thinking. The soul of paradox illustrates that both true opinion and beyond right thinking can be real at the same time.

Our usual understanding of a paradox is that it is a contradiction.

As words evolved, it was recognized that two facts which appear opposite or contrary can both be real at the same time. A human being is a perfect example of paradox. It is said that we are made in the image and likeness of the Divine, yet we also inhabit a finite, physical form.

"The sentences…being strong on both sides, are equivocal." Shakespeare

We all come from the same infinite Source.

"There are no whole truths. All truths are half-truths. It is trying to treat them as whole truths that pays the devil." Alfred North Whitehead

"A double meaning shows double sense." Hood

This semantic source of paradox brings a clear focus to the possibilities that lie beyond our human belief systems, to the acceptance and respect for different ways of thinking and being.

144

"The passion for truth is silenced by answers which have the weight of undisputed authority." Paul Tillich

"Do I contradict myself? Very well, then I contradict myself, I am large, I contain multitudes." Walt Whitman

Have you ever felt pulled in two directions at the same time? When was the last time you felt this way? What aspect of this dilemma did you find confusing? What did you learn from it? How can recognizing the existence of paradox help you to increase your acceptance of differing opinions and points of view? Can you now see paradox as an intriguing dance of opposites that permeates all that exists?

shadow

Shadow is derived from the Old English *scead*, and from the Greek *skotos*, meaning shade or comparative darkness. Shadow, therefore, is a space sheltered from direct light, but paradoxically caused or created by the light.

Shadow reminds us that there is a part of us, hidden from our own view, that we often deny or that we want to remain veiled. A shadow is only a dark reflection with no substance of its own. The soul of this word brings to our attention that the 'shadow' part of us originates from light.

"Every problem contains the seeds of its own solution." Stanley Arnold

Carl Jung has written extensively about our shadow side, a subject that continues to interest many writers, therapists, and those seeking counsel. According to Jung, we all have a shadow side that we do not acknowledge or may be totally unaware of. These shadows can take the form of challenging relationships with others or negative thoughts leading to activities that are less than admirable. Shadows can be seen as positive wake-up calls that move us to discover the highest in ourselves. When we become willing to face these negative or painful shadows, we may be very surprised to uncover our life's purpose or our innate genius following us in a subdued light.

Astronomer and physicist Galileo (1564-1642) was the father of the heliocentric model of our solar system. He observed shadows and changes in shadows over time which led him to hypothesize that the earth rotates around the sun. Such a new idea was not only contrary to the prevailing Aristotelian theories but also considered heretical. His is a very real example of how literally the gifts inherent within the shadows can bring about ingenious discoveries.

"Genius, in truth, means little more than the faculty of perceiving in an unhabitual way." William James

Shadow has so many meanings or interpretations. Some of the common usages are—the scary shadows of night; an imaginary vision; a protective cover or shelter; the shadow casting gloom; a specter; a spy; someone always by your side; the description of a person, like 'a shadow of the former self,' and so on.

Since shadows are mostly associated with darkness, they are a phenomenon produced by and dependent on light. We might say that our shadows complete us when they fulfill their missions to enlighten our souls. When this happens we come to the realization that our true nature is this light. Each soul who realizes the reality of its true nature contributes to the enlightenment of our entire world. This happens after we have faced and transformed the dark forces in ourselves which are expressed as negative behavior patterns.

Do you have a conscious awareness of your shadow? If so, how did it get your attention? Was anyone else involved? Were you able to accept the revelation and how did it resolve itself? Did it lead to any life changes? In the future, do you think you can discover more insights or gifts from these experiences? How can this new understanding improve your life?

simplicity

Simplicity is derived from the Latin words *plex* and *simplex*, meaning fold or one fold, single rather than manifold. Simplicity therefore focuses on a singleness of heart.

The soul of simplicity indicates that less is sometimes better than more. We often hear ourselves and others say, "I wish life could be simpler," or "I am so tired of...." In the rush and hustle of everyday life, even the simple tasks seem to become more and more complicated, frustrating, and wearing on the body and spirit. This is true in spite of all of our timesaving technological advances, and sometimes it appears to happen *because* of them.

"Simplicity is an exact medium between too little and too much." Sir Joshua Reynolds

One of the slogans of Alcoholics Anonymous is, "Keep it simple." It is wise to focus on one thing at a time, even though it takes many steps and much effort for our plans to come to fruition.

"A man must be able to cut a knot, for everything cannot be untied; he must know how to disengage what is essential from the detail in which it is enwrapped, for everything cannot be equally considered; in a word, he must be able to simplify his duties, his business, and his life." Henri Frederic Amiel

Many express feelings such as this at tax time each year! Deciphering and trying to keep abreast of the myriad tax laws that are constantly changing can be vexing and exhausting. Surely there must be a way that this out-of-control business aspect of our lives could be simplified! Some try to control it in part by keeping careful and updated records that make it simpler and less complicated at the year's end.

"Making the simple complicated is commonplace; making the complicated simple, awesomely simple, that's creativity." Charles Mingus

The next time you think you want more of anything, ask yourself if it is really necessary, and if the wish is granted how it will affect your life? Will your life then be simpler and more satisfying? Listen to what the quiet voice of simplicity, deep within, has to say. Is there wisdom for you in that voice?

"There is no greatness where there is no simplicity." Tolstoy

The success of the renowned songwriter Irving Berlin has been attributed to a simple philosophy of life—to affirm rather then complain, to express kindness rather than despair.

"The great artists and thinkers are the simplifiers." Henri Frederic Amiel

Have you ever associated simplicity with having less? Are there things that you can eliminate from your activities or possessions that will make your life less complex and more peaceful?

suffering

Suffering is derived from the Latin *ferre* and from the Greek *phereim*, meaning to bear, to carry, or to endure. Suffering conveys the idea of the holding of something that is heavy or difficult.

Modern technology has made it possible for us to be bombarded daily with graphic depictions of human misery. It is hard to turn away from such images and resume life in a "normal" way.

Pain of all kinds is an inevitable part of life. Yet pain can be distinguished from suffering in that to suffer is often to be resigned to a painful situation over which the individual has little or no control, and with little hope of relief or change.

Some have a different view of suffering. For instance, many Buddhists see the root of all suffering as attachment or clinging. St. Paul tells us that suffering produces endurance. Dr. Brugh Joy observes what he calls "the mystery of suffering" as a doorway for transformation, a path to transcending the ordinary, and an opening to the mystery of compassion. The experience of suffering often prompts a personal inventory or reevaluation that can result in important changes and the rearrangement of priorities. Thus, it can either embitter us or provide the opportunity for hidden gifts to unfold.

An Arab proverb asks the question, "How many opportunities present themselves to a man without his noticing them?"

"It is by those who have suffered that the world has been advanced." Leo Tolstoy

It is generally accepted that anyone who is experiencing difficult circumstances is thought to be suffering. On the other hand, we can also look at suffering as a concept that can be used to frame any adverse or painful experience. While the emotions and/or physical pain we feel is real, it doesn't necessarily become "suffering" until we allow our emotions to create a drama around the situation. If this drama is a coping mechanism we turn to in order to help us through trying times, it can be useful in the short term. However, if it is allowed to continue after the crisis passes, it can become a detrimental force in our lives. It is possible for us to eventually let go of the heavy load of our stories and dramas and thus accept our life circumstances and fashion a more empowered and peaceful way of life.

What would happen if we asked people who carry out violent actions, directed at individuals, institutions, or countries, to tell us what suffering and pain they are enduring which could prompt these desperate and horrifying acts?

Can we listen in depth to the suffering of others? Can we find ways to help alleviate suffering in all forms, while continuing to put a stop to intentionally harmful or unacceptable acts?

"Whoever is spared personal pain must feel himself called to help in diminishing the pain of others. We must all carry our share of the misery which lies upon the world." Albert Schweitzer

Author Eckhart Tolle calls the widespread suffering that is now being experienced globally the result of a collective insanity, a manifestation of the human condition. However, a new state of consciousness is arising, and both are happening at the same time.

Can we become conscious that we are more than our stories and dramas of suffering? Do you ever find that your troubles contain within them both the learning and the resources with which to overcome them? As we find some peace and serenity in our own healing we can be inspired to find visionary ways to bring healing to suffering wherever it is found.

"We can walk through the darkest night with the radiant conviction that all things work together for the good." Martin Luther King

"The greatest and most important problems of life are all in a certain sense insoluble. They can never be solved, but only outgrown." Carl Jung

Have you ever felt burdened with a heavy load of difficulties? What was happening? How did you respond? How do you respond to the suffering of others?

surrender

Surrender is derived from the Latin *reddere*, meaning to give back again. It thus connotes a 'letting go' in order to return.

Normally we think of surrender as concerning one who has been fighting and eventually gives up, perhaps to be taken prisoner or to be killed. However, according to the soul of the word, surrender means to return to where we came from, our life's Source. This implies a relinquishment of direction to an authority and power within us that is paradoxically at the same time greater than ourselves. This can enable us to both plan and to energetically move in positive directions in life.

Whenever our egoic mind feels fearful and clouded, or we find ourselves in difficult situations, disagreements, or conflicts, we can call on and activate the quiet and reasonable Divine consciousness that lies dormant within us. When we let go of our preconceptions about the outcome and a sense of urgency, we can often discover that higher and better resolutions result. In Alcoholics Anonymous it is called 'surrendering to the will of a higher power.' We reach a point, unique to each person, where we know we need help and are humble enough to ask for it. This frequently happens on our knees.

Often there are no quick fixes or immediate solutions to a difficult problem; therefore, one would hope for a time to reflect, reconsider, or pray, waiting for a change in attitude or

153

for clarity before making choices about a proper response in a particular situation. In the Christian faith, it is the petition to God, 'Thy will be done.' Others attain the same result by accepting that the highest good for all concerned will manifest. When we surrender our worries and concerns it then becomes possible for the Divine to heal our life's situation. Otherwise, the ego can engender a persistent need to control that is born of fear and which can prevent loving, balanced, and even miraculous results from occurring. This blocks our highest good from taking form in our lives.

"The intellect has little to do on the road to discovery. There comes a leap in consciousness, call it intuition or what you will, and the solution comes to you and you don't know how or why." Albert Einstein

Our positive thoughts and our dreams in themselves can be a form of guidance. Sometimes our hopes and desires guide us as well. It is extremely gratifying when the validity of such enlightened insight and guidance is affirmed by good solutions and resolutions through our experience. However, this is not always the case. It may be helpful to trust that there is always a reason for everything even if we can't see it at the time. This act of trust emerges from developing a profound sense of humility as we encounter the depth of life's mystery.

"Time will change and even reverse many of your present opinions. Refrain, therefore, awhile from setting yourself up as a judge of the highest matters." Plato

Think back to a time when you surrendered and received Divine guidance in a difficult situation, or even in ordinary decision-making. What was happening and how did it turn out? Then recall a time when you simply reacted without surrendering. Do you find that better, more balanced decisions are made and that positive action results when you are willing to ask for and receive higher guidance?

wait

Wait is derived originally from the Latin word *uigere*, meaning to be in good health or vigorous. Later, wait became the medieval English *waiten*, meaning watchman. The soul of wait therefore implies that watching or being on guard is necessary for our health and strength.

In today's world, we normally think of waiting as unpleasant, annoying, or at best an exercise in the cultivation of patience. Yet, the source of wait indicates that it may be a time to be cognizant of our thoughts and emotions, to determine whether or not they are contributing to our health and strength, or discern where they are taking us.

A Chinese proverb says, "With time and patience the mulberry leaf becomes a silk gown."

Are you waiting for something better to happen? Do you find yourself in a state of discontent as you stand and wait in a line? The soul of wait is an important reminder that we can begin to see even this very common experience, which often tests our patience, in a positive, life-enhancing way.

"Patience is a bitter plant, but it has sweet fruit." Old Proverb

One thing you may find helpful would be to shift your attitude to one of concentration on anything and everything that contributes to your well-being. We can overcome the very idea of waiting by centering on the fact that we can just be, in any and all moments, believing that every moment is precious. For instance, if you happen to be waiting in a grocery check-out line, you might focus on how fortunate you are to have access to such plentiful, healthy, tasty food and that you have the freedom to pick and choose what to purchase, or express gratitude to those working there.

"There are no shortcuts to Heaven, only the ordinary way of ordinary things." Vincent McNabb

If you are in a special hurry while waiting to be served or in grid lock traffic and begin to feel some annoyance, it might help to take a deep breath in order to shift to a place of acceptance in that very moment. Perhaps then you can catch a glimpse of the joy of just 'being' fully in the present. Waiting can even be seen as an opportunity to recharge your energy or to give another person, who appears to be in a huge hurry, your place in the line. Enjoy the look of surprise on their faces and the different reactions that you receive from others, as a result. Such a small act of consideration can contribute to your own spiritual well-being and health as well.

"People in a hurry cannot think, cannot grow, nor can they decay. They are preserved in a state of perpetual puerility." Eric Hoffer

When was the last time you had to wait for something to happen or stood in a line? What was happening? Where were you? How did it feel? What was your reaction? In the future, will you be able to be more content while you wait?

wealth

Wealth is derived from the old English *wela*, meaning to be well, and from the Medieval English *weal*, meaning well-being. The soul of wealth therefore has to do with our health.

"The first wealth is health." Ralph Waldo Emerson

We are often told that good health is worth more than gold. In Old English, wealth became *commonweal* or *commonwealth*. Commonwealth meant health and happiness, but the measure of happiness came to be interpreted as meaning only monetary wealth. The poor, and also the wealthy, believed that happiness could be purchased.

There are those who assert that there is an abundance of wealth to go around in this world. If this is true, then why is there such inequity connected with the distribution of this wealth? The rich only seem to get richer while the poor get poorer. It certainly is true that it takes money to buy food and shelter, unless we live close to the land, where it is assumed we can raise our food and build our own housing, as pioneers did.

"We can have democracy in this country or we can have great wealth concentrated in the hands of a few, but we can't have both." Louis D. Brandeis

As the soul of this word says, wealth includes and deals with far more than just money. Do you find that your health and well-being include not only bodily and mental health, but also the health of spirit and conscience; work that is satisfying; creative and caring relationships; a close-knit and loving family; a vision and awareness of that which gives life real meaning and purpose, and whatever else contributes in a positive way to your life?

My experience is that well-being and real wealth are primarily rooted in a deep awareness of being connected to God. The Creator deeply fulfills all of my needs and knows what they are before I ask. The wealthier I feel, the more wealth I have to give away. It is circular!

"It is impossible to outgive God. Miracles happen when we give." Anonymous

One thing that may help us if we ever entertain the thought that we do not have enough, or that there is not enough to go around, is to make a gratitude list. Such a list makes it clear just how wealthy we are! Can the realization that we are in fact all wealthy heirs of our Creator result in behavior that is generous, loving, compassionate, and forgiving?

"The human race has had long experience and a fine tradition in surviving adversity. But we now face a task for which we have little experience, the task of surviving prosperity." Alan Gregg

"Enough is as good as a feast." John Haywood

What makes you feel wealthy? What contributes to your feelings of well-being? How are the two, wealth and health, related in your life? What past relationships and activities have contributed the most to your well-being? How can you expand on that now?

PART FOUR

TRANSFORMATION

It is one of the most mysterious and impressive of all of nature's displays, and yet it is one of the most silent. A humble, creeping caterpillar wraps itself in a cocoon and emerges a dazzling butterfly! Is a caterpillar the same as a butterfly? No. Is a butterfly just a caterpillar with wings? No. Yet nothing entered or left the sealed cocoon while the metamorphosis was underway. Change and transformation are awesome forces of nature, and they act on all of us as surely as upon the caterpillar inside the cocoon. The process of transformation is often arduous, spontaneous and unexpected. It occurs whether we want it to or not. One of the strangest and most frightening works of 20th century literature is Franz Kafka's *The Metamorphosis*. Kafka's character Gregor Samsa awakens to find himself transformed into an insect. Kafka drew on bizarre exaggeration to make his point. Have you ever 'awakened' to discover you were someone or something you weren't before? A parent. An employ-er. A patient. In this section, we will consider the words space, spirituality, energy, and flowers. We will also examine other words that are part of the process of transformation and that can contribute to it—crisis, courage, and humility.

The word time is also included in this section, for time underlies everything. We are not static beings. We are beings in time and time is always flowing. At different moments in our lives, we may be more acutely aware of the flow of time and that it is against that background all of our transformation occurs.

St. Augustine recalls in his autobiography the prayer he offered as a young man having a lot of fun and not very interested in "being good"—"Dear God, help me to aban-don my evil ways and follow your teachings—but not yet." Expected or not, transformation and change are constants in our lives. Give thought to the concepts embedded in the souls of the words in this section and see how they apply to the transformation you are experiencing in your own life. Ultimately, we are not powerless to change our lives, for we have the ability to harness the forces of transformation to become whatever we desire and to take us wherever we want to go. All of the words in this part of the book are important, but above all don't overlook the word, dream.

addiction

The word *addict* comes from the Latin, addicere, a legal term that means being bound to a sentence by a court. In contemporary usage, an addict is the prisoner of a habit.

Addiction refers to any activity performed by someone despite the fact that they know they are acting against their own interest, their well-being and even risking their actual physical existence.

The behavior of individuals chemically dependent on both legal and illegal substances is more easily noticed, documented and prosecuted than the more subtle addictions the general population employs by abusing things used by all of us in our ordinary daily activities. These can include eating, shopping, patterns of difficult relationships, and numerous other habits that can be destructive to ourselves and others. Many of these actions begin as an attempt to escape from painful and unpleasant life situations and feelings which are difficult to face or in some cases even identify. How can anyone in this state know they need help, much less have the ability to obtain it?

The soul of this word makes it clear that an addict is "bound," but it does not mean that an individual must be bound to something harmful or destructive. In fact, the pure definition of addiction leads us to believe that we can just as easily be bound to something of a highly positive nature.

161

"Habit is a cable: we weave a thread of every day, and at last we cannot break it." Horace Mann

The positive connotation of the word addiction is a far cry from the customary negative note surrounding its popular usage referring to people addicted to drugs. In fact, I have seen addicts in recovery become actual lifesavers to others as they open up and verbalize in non-threatening settings. This occurs after humbling themselves by surrendering and reaching out for help, usually after many tries and failures. Having experienced love and support, they no longer need to be bound over to fears, insecurities and feelings of unworthiness that caused them to search for love and acceptance through self-destructive behaviors. Rather, new practices are formed based on responsibility and the sharing of the true loving nature they have discovered in themselves. Courageous personal victories are happening in our midst everyday.

The amazing and wonderful feats of bravery, courage, and human concern that we witnessed on 9/11, by all those who risked or gave their lives for others, must have come from positive habits those individuals formed over many years prior to that sad event. Throughout human history, we have seen that habits of all kinds have had both positive and negative outcomes.

Numerous people have told me that when they realized that their true nature is love, positive self-respecting habits were the natural result. The favorite habit of many, including myself, is a prayer and meditation time each day, preferably in the morning. This solitude creates the space for our minds to be cleared and thought patterns to be transformed. It nurtures the ability to face pain and difficulties and move beyond them. The result is often a more peaceful, loving attitude with which to meet the day. The peace that we experience then spills over into the lives of all those with whom we have contact.

Take time to look at your own life to see what you are in the 'habit' of doing. What activities do you consider to be rewarding and positive? Which ones do you consider to be negative or destructive? What is motivating you when you indulge in your habits? Why do you allow them in your life? Do you act them out alone or with others? Are there some habits that you want to replace with new and more positive ones? Can you imagine what your life would be like if you did so?

angels

Entire books have been written on the subject of angels, a word derived from the Latin *angelos*, meaning messengers.

"The highest function of mind is its function of messenger." D.H. Lawrence

The word message is derived from *mittere*, meaning mission. Since everyone and everything that exists has a life mission, and angels are messengers with missions, then different layers of angels must be everywhere and in everyone; in all of nature, the animal kingdom, history, art of all kinds, dreams, ideas, clouds, omens, and on and on, in whatever way you can think of or name—even in a name itself.

Often, angels that we label 'good' or 'bad' have been depicted in art and words in a supernatural, dualistic way, as though they are always outside of us. Many of us have experienced what we call 'guardian angels' that seem to come from another realm and who protect us from impending dangers and woes of all kinds. The attention of these guardians, however, never interferes with our free will to make choices.

Although messenger angels sometimes come to us from unfamiliar realms, they awaken us with messages important for our daily lives that we can in turn share with others. Whether kind or unkind, we are all angels to one another. How would the world be different if we all thought of ourselves as kind and joyful angels?

164

"A single event can awaken within us a stranger totally unknown to us. To live is to be slowly born." Antoine de Saint-Exupery

What we may consider to be insane, sick, destructive happenings can be messages serving to show us something we need to be aware of. Likewise, what we think of as positive or negative messages may be angelic wake-up calls from the Divine. "Waking up" may come gradually or it can come in a sudden, dramatic moment.

Has the word angel, therefore, been given too many boundaries? If everything is a divine message and everyone is a divine messenger (the agreed meaning of the word angel), then there are no limits to life's angelic possibilities.

Try now to find messages and messengers in your own life. Just allow yourself to be in a relaxed state and think of a time in your early life when a messenger came to you. Think back to grade school, then to high school, perhaps on to college, professional, vocational school. Now look at yesterday and see where any messages might be. Who were the messengers? What did they share, and most importantly, how did they try to communicate their message?

Did you ever have an angelic experience in your childhood? If so, where did this happen, how did it happen, and with whom did it happen? What role did words have in this experience? Think of other situations from your life that symbolize angelic interventions. Try writing what comes to you and let your writing lead the way as you describe them. It may take you beyond ego to the Divine and you may discern God speaking to you in what comes through your writing or guided thoughts. Your Creator is patiently waiting for you at this moment.

Can you see yourself as a receiver and a giver of angelic messages this very day?

change

The word change is derived from the Latin *cambiare*, meaning 'to bend.' Change, therefore, is constant bending or transformation.

"There is nothing permanent except change." Heraclitus

In the words of Evelyn Waugh, "Change is the only evidence of life."

As we know, if something cannot bend, it is almost certain to break.

We are told by the scientific cosmic inflation theory that everything is constantly changing, expanding, evolving, becoming. This phenomenon has been called the 'music of creation' by scientists at the University of California, Berkeley. It is obvious that life itself is a constant process of change, yet it seems that we largely fear transformation and often resist it.

However, it is our internal transformation that is needed in order to bring about the changes that we want to see happen in our outer world. No force from the outside has ever put a stop to hatred or racism, for instance. If we want to see more love and peace encircling us, is it possible that we need to embrace the chaos that always precipitates important change?

Ramsay Clark stated that, "Turbulence is life force. It is opportunity. Let's love turbulence and use it for change."

Trees are a prime example of change as they go through a recurring process of life and metamorphosis year after year. They change in size and strength as they share their pollen and seeds for growing new saplings and so ably and graciously bend to accommodate the present moment, forever changing month after month. Just think, trees are never the same as the previous week, month, or years, but always maintain their individuality and identity. They, like us, are 'beings' of change. Throughout the seasons deciduous trees exhibit the natural, life-giving nature of change.

"Wherever we are, it is but a stage on the way to somewhere else, and whatever we do, however well we do it, it is only a preparation to do something else that shall be different." Robert Louis Stevenson

As our consciousness is raised or changed, the world around us will also change.

"All changes, even the most longed for, have their melancholy, for what we leave behind us is a part of ourselves; we must die to one life before we can enter into another." Anatole France

Ralph Waldo Emerson said in his famous essay on Self-Reliance: "A foolish consistency is the hobgoblin of little minds."

When you were a child what made you conscious of the lack of permanence? What did it feel like? When did other insights about change come to you? What was transpiring in your life at the time? Was there maturing or growth involved? Was fear involved when you found yourself resistant to change? How can you become more comfortable with the constant change that life inevitably brings?

compassion

The word compassion is derived from the word *patience* or the Latin, *pati*, meaning to show leniency, and from the Late Latin *compati*, meaning to suffer with.

Traits in our daily lives that are associated with compassion are thoughtfulness, understanding, kindness, concern and helpfulness. In addition to those words, according to the soul of compassion, we are called to look deeply at the qualities of patience and leniency. The attributes of tolerance, serenity and a freedom from prejudice can often result from this practice.

"There is nothing bitter that a patient mind cannot find some solace for it." Marcus Annaeus Seneca

There is an old saying that unhurt people would never be much good in the world. We might add that all human beings are hurt or suffer in some way by virtue of being in this physical form. The derivation of compassion conveys this same truth: if we didn't experience pain in our lives, there would be no way to empathize with or respond to the pain or suffering of others. We can, of course, to some degree feel and have compassion for others as we become aware of their plight; however, a real depth of true compassion, and the patience that accompanies it, can only come with a firsthand experience of what others have to face and endure.

"The race of mankind would perish did they cease to aid each other. We cannot exist without mutual help." Sir Walter Scott

Most faiths and spiritual traditions suggest that we try to provide for others what we wish to experience ourselves, and most of us want to be treated with the patience that is associated with compassion. We long to experience the love and kindness associated with leniency.

Jack Kornfield writes that, "Loving kindness gives birth to a natural compassion. The compassionate heart holds the pain and sorrow of our life and of all beings with mercy and tenderness."

It is not possible to be loving, kind, or compassionate toward others unless we are first aware of our own value and, as a result, treat ourselves with respect and loving benevolence. The more tender our own hearts become to ourselves, the more they reach out to others.

"It is this tender heart that has the power to transform the world." Chogyam Trungpa

The next time we lose patience with ourselves or with another, we can recall how we each live and act according to our level of awareness or view of the world, and are usually doing the best we can under our particular circumstances. In our daily conversations with others, whatever we hear or say, we can ask ourselves if the words spoken are harsh and critical or wise and compassionate.

This is important because words have impact (energy), and this released energy comes back to us in kind at some time.

"All altruism springs from putting yourself in the other person's place." Harry Emerson Fosdick

Recall the first time that you felt the stirring of compassion and empathy for another. If it is comfortable for you, describe in writing what was happening and how you felt. Were feelings of leniency with your own shortcomings involved? Did patience play a part? Have you been the recipient of compassion from others? How were you empowered by this experience? Did it help you move through your feelings of pain, guilt, or distress? Did it feel as though you were given a gift? Try to visualize what the world would be like if the deep meaning of the word compassion became a reality. How can you be more compassionate with yourself?

cooperation

The word cooperation is derived from the word *opera* or from the Latin *opus*, meaning work, as a result of an intentional attitude of 'joining together' on the part of many, in order to bring about an even greater work.

We regularly think of cooperation as more than one person acting or working together, but rarely do we notice the 'opera' in the word with all the joint effort and unity that such an image includes.

An opera, for example, is an art form for which many can be given credit and a work that will outlast its composer/author's lifetime. The composer, producer, singers, choreographers, conductor, and members of the orchestra, costume makers, wardrobe keepers, stage and scenery engineers, lighting and sound experts, and last but not least, the production manager(s) are all crucial components for the operatic event. The unqualified cooperation of this diverse company of people and talent is required for a performance to happen and to be a success.

When all of these parts come together cooperatively, they create a magnificent musical drama called opera.

The cooperation required to produce an opera is one of a variety of metaphors for life. Consider the many unique gifts and contributions from all those who organize and perform in our life's opera. The more we express our unique individuality the more we can appreciate the unique gifts of others, or see how we all become diminished unless we encourage and support one another. The overall production is greater than the individual parts, but also dependent on each part. In life, conflicts and disagreements are inevitable; however, it is possible for them to be resolved in an atmosphere of cooperation.

Rudyard Kipling wrote, "I shall know that your good is mine; ye shall know that my strength is yours."

How often do we as individuals cooperate with what we know is for our highest good, let alone transfer that energy to a group action? Loving, cooperative, intelligent activity is something that we need to establish in our own lives if we wish to see it reflected in the greater world.

Take a moment to remember an experience in which all people involved cooperated to achieve a greater good. What was happening and how did it feel? What other times in your life have you felt the same? How has it affected your relationships with others? Do you ever sense that you are a part of a great composition, such as an opera? If so, do you see ways in which your contribution is of vital importance?

courage

The word courage is derived from the Medieval Latin *cordialis*, meaning 'of the heart' or 'intimate,' and thus refers to an intimate energy or spirit that comes from the heart.

How often do we think of courage as an intimate emotion? We are accustomed to thinking of love as intimate, but courage often seems to be something that must come from outside us; a magical force that suddenly arrives to strengthen us and to allay our fears. The semantic source of courage reminds us that its lifesaving energy does have root within us, in the very same place that love resides.

The intimate emotion of love is intrinsic, and it comes from the same 'image of God' which is love itself, residing with every person. Each of us is eternally 'one' with the image of God and can never be separated from that love. The knowledge of this truth is necessary for us to love and accept ourselves. In the Bible we are told, in fact, to love our selves and our neighbors in like manner.

"Ultimately, love is self approval." Sondra Ray

When our hearts are open, we feel connected to one another and we are moved to share love with others in abundant and courageous ways. This loving, intimate courage takes over in spite of the vulnerability and fear that accompany risk.

173

"Courage is rightly esteemed the first of human qualities because it is the quality which guarantees all others." Winston Churchill

We experience courage when we accept and allow the highest aspect of ourselves to push through our fears in order to assist us in overcoming difficulties and attaining great accomplishments. This courage enables us to embark on new and sometimes risky undertakings in life, such as a career change or the breaking of a harmful habit.

When a young person becomes aware that an attitude or activity of their peer group may not be in his or her best interest, it takes courage to overcome the powerful fear of the peer group's rejection. This same fear of rejection is what drives groups of people throughout all levels of society to form collectives which they hope will help protect them from other groups. The deep-seated instinct to belong is pervasive in all societies and cultures, and violence and chaos escalate as these groups collide. A powerful courage must issue forth from everyone in order for this endless cycle to be broken and transformed.

"Courage is the energy of the infinite that slips through the door of an open soul and into the world." Stephanie Ariel Marsh

Do you feel you have this type of courageous connection? If so, on what occasions did that connection surface? What were your feelings during those times? What did you do to demonstrate that courage? How has it affected your life?

crisis

Crisis is derived from the Greek words *krisis*, meaning a sifting or a decisive moment, and from *kritikos*, meaning the ability to discern.

A crisis can be small-scale or more monumental, a marriage, the birth of a child, or death of a loved one. Many events, both positive and negative, are times of crisis. These pivotal moments can be very painful and unsettling, raising basic questions about life's meaning and purpose. They can be opportunities to sift out and discern what is really important in life and to awaken our hearts. We can gradually become aware of what matters to us as we feel our hearts gain wisdom and as we see what we have sifted out and replaced.

"The central problem of our age is how to act decisively in the absence of certainty." Bertrand Russell

The experience of a crisis, with its necessary choices, inherently includes uncertainty and danger, along with the opportunity for change. We usually refer to a crisis in life as a time of tragedy or intense pressure, but the root of this word demonstrates that all crises can be times of decision which present opportunities for new insights and positive changes.

"When written in Chinese, the word crisis is composed of two characters—One represents danger and the other represents opportunity." John F. Kennedy

Planet Earth today faces unparalleled danger and along with it the greatest of opportunities to establish understanding and peace. This time of crisis is full of uncertainty, yet to gain perspective we can look back in human history at how the uncertainties of every age kept our world in a constant state of crisis.

"The quest for certainty blocks the search for meaning. Uncertainty is the very condition to impel man to unfold his powers." Eric Fromm

"Times of general calamity and confusion have ever been productive of the greatest minds. The purest one is produced from the hottest furnace, and the brightest thunderbolt is elicited from the darkest storms." Charles Caleb Colton

Think of a time of crisis that was in retrospect a turning point in your own life, a watershed moment. Was it a time to sift through the bits and pieces of life that were uncomfortable, uncertain, and unexplored? It takes courage to allow the light to shine into all the dark corners. Can you remember a critical decision that you made as a result of that process? How does that change affect your life today?

dream

Dream is derived from the old High German, *traum*, meaning to deceive and from the Medieval English, *dreme*, meaning joy.

Dreams can be either premonitions of the future or they can educate us to help us deal with troubling life experiences. They can also bring to our conscious awareness issues we need to pay attention to or work on. Either way, dreams are gifts that come from deep within our unconscious to benefit us.

An old Jewish proverb suggests, "A dream uninterpreted is like a letter unread."

Dreams are messages that can help us to sort out our past and to imagine our future. They deal with the full range of feelings that we experience every day. Some dream analysts suggest that we can even choose to have happy or unhappy dreams.

"The most difficult thing in life is to know yourself." Thales

Even our so-called daydreams deserve to be taken to heart as pictures of what we hope will happen next or of where we wish to be, rather than where we find ourselves at a given moment.

"We haven't found enough dreams. We haven't dreamed enough." Georgia O'Keeffe

There are no good dreams or bad dreams, only dreams that tell us different parts of the truth about our mysterious existence. The symbolism in our dreams during sleep can expand our awareness in uncensored ways and give us personal guidance. Whether they are the dreams that we experience during sleep, our meditations, or our daydreams, each can give us lessons, principles, and insights that help us with our most important work, which is to know ourselves in a more objective way. The significance of dreams varies according to our interpretation of them.

"Reach high, for stars lie hidden in your soul. Dream deep, for every dream precedes the goal." Pamela Vaull Starr

During our waking life, which we usually consider to be "reality," there is ample opportunity to creatively practice the insights given to us in our dreams. These insights have the potential to move us to higher levels of consciousness and understanding. It follows that dreams have the power to transform our lives and world.

"If you do not ask yourself what it is you know, you will go on listening to others and change will not come because you will not hear your own truth." St. Bartholomew

Do you pay attention to or examine your dreams? What do you learn from them? Do you receive guidance from your interpretation of the symbols found there? What emotions or revelations have been revealed to you that were not in your conscious awareness before? Do you receive insights that could not have come any other way? Can you see how being in touch with your dreams can guide you to the fulfillment of your goals and aspirations?

Easter

In Anglo-Saxon English, the pagan word Easter, *eostre*, meaning goddess of spring, celebrates the renewal of life after the deadness of winter, and it has been retained for the Christian festival of the Resurrection of Christ.

In most European languages this Christian Easter is called Passover, taken from the Jewish Passover. For example, in French—*Pacques,* and in Italian—*Pasqua.* These words, like all words, point to something that the scribes through their mythological interpretations have attempted to express, a great truth that was for them very real and has continued to be real through the ages. The words symbolize the birth of Christianity over two thousand years ago.

Most of the symbols of the Jerusalem Easter can be seen in the Jewish celebration of the Tabernacles. The various biblical narratives of the Resurrection of Jesus were told in that legendary setting. Even though these legends consist of symbols from the past, it doesn't mean they should be dismissed as untrue. The fact that Jesus is a living reality in the lives of so many is proof enough that the Easter moment was and continues to be real and live in the hearts of those who practice Christianity.

Easter comes in the Spring as a shining season of light and newness. Just as dawn comes in the East to awaken and enliven the earth, Eastertide likewise brings a renewal to the earth that restores hope.

Have you noticed in the Spring how the dogwood trees first burst with buds, then come the flowers, representatives of the return of new life that all of nature undergoes?

"Deep in their roots, all flowers keep the light." Theodore Roethke

Many have told me how regeneration has come in their lives in a variety of ways, from the healing of a physical or psychological wound to the opening of new doors of opportunity when others were hopelessly shut. Some call these happenings 'their Easter experiences'!

"Relying on God has to begin all over again every day as if nothing had yet been done." C.S. Lewis

"Easter is not a time for groping through dusty, musty tomes or tombs to disprove spontaneous generation or even to prove life eternal. It is a day to fan the ashes of dead hope, a day to banish doubts and seek the slopes where the sun is rising, to revel in the faith which transports us out of ourselves and the dead past into the vast and inviting unknown." Lewiston

What are your deepest recollections of Easter experiences, or deepest recollections of renewal, whether it fell at Easter or not? Do you draw inspiration from nature's seasonal cycles? If so, when and how? What gift does each season share with you?

energy

The word energy comes from the Greek *ergon* and means an active force. It refers to the force that moves us to act.

We usually think of energy as that which is generated by the corporate power companies that supply our electricity. However, as the root of the word indicates, we are in our essence a powerful energy force.

Our bodies are described by science as 'solid' because the body vibrates at certain high frequencies of energy that results in density. The higher our vibrations, the healthier are our bodies.

"While the cause is hidden, the force is very well known." Ovid

Our thoughts and feelings are thrust into motion or action by the powerful energy of our emotions. It follows that if we do not use our energy to build our life intentionally, we will witness it happening randomly from the energy generated by our unconscious thoughts. Energy equals e-motion (energy in motion), and the most elegant use of emotion is its service in bringing our creations into being.

Carolyn Myss, in her book *Energy Anatomy*, describes the human energy system and how we can choose to be in partnership with the energetic Divine power to heal our bodies, minds, and activities. She shows how our inner unconscious forces bring us challenges with relationships, money, and many other issues of life.

The energy force of both our conscious and unconscious thoughts and emotions is extremely powerful indeed. Energy follows thought and is the fuel that creates the world around us.

Psychiatrist John MacCallum writes, "We all agree that we are made up of energy and matter and maybe to that list I would like to add a healing energy or healing consciousness and I might call it love. ...I would like to define it at least as something that is non-local...that can go anywhere...something that is not related to time. ...We have all kinds of evidence to support the notion that love is an innate capability of living beings...ultimately we have to call it some kind of energy."

Are you consciously directing the creative energy of your life? Does your outer life reflect what your conscious mind desires? If not, can you bring the unconscious thoughts and feelings responsible for those results to awareness? What happens when you replace these with positive energy?

flower

The word flower is derived from the Late Latin *flores* and from the Latin *mensturi fluroes*, meaning monthly flowings. Do you ever associate flowers and humans as being connected in the same mysterious and amazing cycle of life? The root of the word seemingly connects them through the 'monthly flowings' without which there would be no life.

Further, there is a real connection between flowering plants and those individuals who have awakened to a higher consciousness. Perhaps the main difference is that these plants that evolved from their earlier non-flowering state to flowering varieties do not possess the power of choice that human beings have.

"And the day came when the risk it took to remain tight inside the bud was more painful than the risk it took to blossom." Anais Nin

Charles Darwin called the search for the origin of flowers an "abominable mystery." In my research, I found that when flowers originated they seemed to appear abruptly and without any connection to earlier non-flowering plants. However, recently scientists from China and the United States found the fossil of the plant *archaefructus*, reported by William Crepet, Chairman of Plant Biology at Cornell University. This is the most primitive flowering plant ever discovered. The *archaefructus* is the aquatic progenitor of today's waterlily. It is estimated that the plant lived in

Northeastern China at least 125 million years ago. A genetic analysis of the waterlily showed that because of its chromosomes it might be the intermediate form linking the flowering plants we know with primitive non-flowering plants.

"The trouble with evolution is that it happens slowly and is seemingly absent of order. It is often confusing, difficult to decipher, devoid of spectacular happenings. As a result, while in progress, evolution seldom makes the front pages or the evening news. Too bad, because it could help us understand what is happening in the world." Warren Brown

With watering, nourishment, and gentle care, both flowers and people blossom and flourish as they evolve through their life cycles. Is it possible that flowers can also develop higher and higher consciousness with each year of bloom? Do you see this blossoming intertwined with their interaction with human beings, and perhaps with animals?

"To me the meanest flower that blooms can give
Thoughts that do often lie too deep for tears."

Wordsworth

Do you ever think what life might be like without the beauty and joy of flowers? Are you aware of how much we depend on vegetation for our life? What has helped you to flower, blossom, or evolve? When did you notice this happening in your life? Who was interacting with you when this occurred and where were you at the time?

heaven

Heaven is derived from *heafan* in Old English, but no meaning is given. Heaven, it follows, is something we know nothing concrete about, even though many imagine heaven as an idyllic haven that awaits us in an afterlife.

In the ancient words of Confucius, "Heaven means to be one with God."

At an audience in Rome several years ago, the Pope, agreeing with Confucius, described hell as the opposite of heaven, or the experience of separation from God—an experience he said we bring on ourselves, thus punishing ourselves.

If these words of Confucius and the Pope are true, is it any wonder that heaven is difficult to define, describe, or imagine? Maybe when we experience love, unity, a peace that passes understanding, or what might be called 'pure joy' we are experiencing some semblance of heaven.

Perhaps religious and other spiritual traditions were established to bridge separations and divisions through the power of consciousness and to foster a heaven-like, harmonious earth. How many of us long to walk across this bridge that has yet to be recognized in earth time? Is it possible that we could build such a bridge ourselves through personal spiritual practices which must include the art of forgiveness?

Dr. Mansukh Patel, author and presenter of an award-winning TV documentary on the Bhagavad Gita who has become known in Europe as 'The Young Ghandi,' has written, "It is not where you are that creates a heaven, but rather who you are, and how much joy you bring to the people around you."

To you, what is heaven? Where did your concept of heaven come from? Would it be helpful to know more about other concepts of heaven? Have you ever experienced something that you would consider to have a heavenly quality? Would you consider inviting a similar experience into your life again?

humility/power

Humility is derived from the Latin *humus*, which means physically of the earth, lowly. Power is derived from the Latin *posse*, which means to be able to act, and from the Latin *potis*, meaning mastery. These two words may seem contradictory, but they are in essence who we are. In fact, it is the balance between these two polarities that results in the satisfactory expression of a human being's life.

As we examine the roots of the words humility and power, we see that they bring together two qualities of our humanity, demonstrating that despite our physical nature, our entire being is filled with the power of ability. Because of the possibilities inherent in this power, as the original word conveys, even the mastery of our thoughts and emotions is feasible.

"Man's capacities have never been measured." Thoreau

With the infinite creative choices that are ours, we have the inherent power to consciously or unconsciously bring about our world's destruction, or to decide to create positive and new ways of being. In the words of Edmund Burke, "The only thing necessary for evil to triumph is for enough good men to do nothing."

Whenever you feel unworthy or overwhelmed by a sense of powerlessness, remember that true humility comes with the acknowledgement that while we are creatures of the dust that have not awakened to all the answers, we are also each a part of a mysterious power in the universe larger than we can imagine or comprehend. A universal power that, when called on, can create, change, and heal with unlimited potential.

"So God created man in his own image, in the image of God created he him." Bible—Genesis 1:27

The light in each person, which is the power of creation, is dimmed by fear. Our inherent greatness can never be realized while we allow fear to control our lives.

Humility is not the doubt of our own power; rather, it is an admission that this power is at work through us, but not owned by us. This consciousness gives us the ability to live within these seemingly opposite attributes, humility/power, that are common to everyone and shared by all.

John Bunyan, famous for his *Pilgrim's Progress*, wrote, "He that is humble, ever shall have God to be his guide."

In what ways are you expressing both your humility and the power you have been given? Do you see everyone you meet as a reflection both of your own humility and your powerful potential?

judgment

Judgment is derived from the Latin *dictum* and the Medieval Latin *judex*, meaning to say, to show, to tell, to point out the law, or to proclaim; an accusatory note came later. Judgment can convey either positive affirmation or harsh criticism and blame today, but originally it simply meant to point out objective facts.

We are constantly evaluating and discriminating in our world. Judgment can be a word that means the use of good sense, wisdom, prudence, perception, insight, or reasoning, but it commonly carries a negative connotation of condemnation.

A scientific study cited by physicist James Goure indicates that the vast majority of all conversations are judgmental. Our judgmental thoughts are so pervasive that we even trick ourselves into thinking they are beneficial. What these judgments actually do is block our love and dim the light in others.

When critical thoughts come into our heads, we can choose not to entertain them. We can choose accepting attitudes that look beyond behavior. Thoughts only have efficacy when we apply the power of our emotions to them. Thus we do not have to be troubled by every random thought that enters our mind. Dismissing any negative thought without emotion as quickly as it appears prevents that thought from becoming a reality.

"Great Spirit, help me never to judge another until I have walked in his moccasins." Sioux Indian Prayer

Since disagreements are inevitable, our challenge is how to conduct 'civil' disagreements! The American judicial system holds a person innocent until proven guilty, founded on the ancient Hebrew meaning of justice. Mishpat is the Hebrew word for judgment, meaning redemption and vindication. In our world, so full of thoughts of unworthiness and guilt leading to ridicule, judgment has taken on a harsher meaning.

It is worth noting that there is within the legal profession a collaboration called the Holistic Bar Association, which promotes creative alternatives to adversarial practice. Its founder, William Zyvaden, calls this method of practicing law "beyond judgment." One holistic practitioner, Peter Gable, builds on Martin Luther King's definition of justice as, "Love correcting that which revolts against love."

Such a concept seeks to promote a legal culture which links justice with empathy and thereby restores wholeness to the parties involved in dispute. South Africa's Truth and Reconciliation Commission is a model Gable uses to begin to redefine the attorney/client and the client/client relationships as a spiritual encounter.

"The strictest justice is sometimes the greatest injustice." Publius Terentius Afer

If we replace the current use of the word judgment with the word assessment, we can create a loving way to allow others to be who they are. In doing so we become discerning about when to set boundaries or to strongly prohibit harmful or inappropriate behavior in ourselves or others.

Imagine making what you deem to be a serious mistake, and consider how you would wish to be treated. Do you think being assessed for your behavior would be more helpful than being judged? Can you see that the positive use of judgment (assessment) may allow for a more effective balanced way of taking responsibility and making amends when deemed necessary?

now

Now is derived from the Medieval English, *nu*, and akin to *new*. We are always aware that now takes place in the present, but we are often oblivious to the newness of the present circumstance.

An adage says, if you have one eye on yesterday and one eye on tomorrow, you're going to be cockeyed today. Can anything ever happen, or has it ever happened, outside of 'now'? It is possible that everything is happening in the eternal 'now.'

"The present is an eternal now." Abraham Cowley

'Now' is gone the moment we experience it. We in fact do live in the world, but are not of it. Just as our bodies recreate themselves minute by minute, are you aware that your soul is also in a process of becoming more and more conscious or 'new'? As this awareness happens, we naturally alter the world around us wherever we are and in whatever we are doing. Effortlessly, our newness is dreamed into being as each moment we are changed in thought, feeling, and action. The past and future are what we want them to be when we acknowledge and allow the newness to unfold.

"A new broom sweeps clean."

"Today, well lived, will prepare me for both the pleasure and the pain of tomorrow." Anonymous

"The moment you enter the Now with your attention, you realize that life is sacred. There is a sacredness to everything you perceive when you are present. The more you live in the Now, the more you sense the simple yet profound joy of Being and the sacredness of life." Eckhart Tolle

"The most important place is here. The most important time is now. The most important person is the one in front of you." Mansukh Patel

Have you ever been aware that you are 'new' every moment? How does it make you feel to be aware that you are 'newness' itself? Does knowing this give you a hopeful and peaceful feeling?

old

Old is derived from the Latin *altus*, meaning nourished, and from the Latin *alescere*, meaning to grow or to grow up. Old therefore implies a full and mature life.

We usually think of 'old people' as weak or infirm, past their prime, and generally going downhill. Yet the soul of this word conveys an innate strength of character and wisdom, with no reference to weakness. Such strength of maturity comes no doubt from an endurance that has been toned through years by innumerable and repeated growth pains and experience.

May Sarton has written, "Old age is not an illness, it is a timeless ascent. As power diminishes, we grow toward more light."

This light of which she speaks comes with the process of maturing and as the result of having had a full and expanding life, with its attending joys and sorrows. It is a light that is not only self-affirming, but also illuminates and warms the lives of others.

"You become mature when you become the authority for your own life." Joseph Campbell

"No wise man ever wished to be younger." Johnathan Swift

One of the goals or purposes of life is to enlighten and nourish other lives. Are we, in fact, sharing with others the benefits of our learning and bestowing blessings as we travel the road to becoming seniors?

"The spiritual eyesight improves as the physical eyesight declines." Plato

"On the day of his death, in his eightieth year, Elliot, 'the Apostle of the Indians,' was found teaching an Indian child at his bedside. 'Why not rest from your labours now?' asked a friend. 'Because,' replied the venerable man, 'I have prayed to God to render me useful in my sphere, and he has heard my prayers; for now that I can no longer preach, he leaves me strength enough to teach this poor child the alphabet." S. Chaplin

Who was the most influential, mature person in your life? How was he or she influential? Can you be more sensitive concerning people of maturity in the future? When you attain your golden years and look back at your life, what would you like to have accomplished? Are you now on that path working toward those accomplishments?

one

_____

One is derived from the Late Latin *unio*, meaning oneness, unity, or union, and from the Latin *universus*,
meaning universal or combined into a whole. According to
its soul, one refers not only to the first number in the scale
of ten, but also to a universal, unifying factor.

Debra Fischer, a member of a team of scientists from
U.C. Berkeley and the Carnegie Institute, describes the discovery of two resonant planets (referred to in the section on
Mystery) that appear to be "humming in harmony, eternally
in sync" as they gravitationally "shepherd each other." Is it
possible that the existence of such an amazing model of oneness and harmony in our universe will encourage earth's people to try and replicate this harmonic energy in unity on our
planet, as the soul of one says? The mere occurrence of such
a phenomenon is a universal sign suggesting that harmony
and unity are primary factors at the heart of the universe.

In this regard, mathematician Steven Stogatz has helped
pioneer a new science, SYNC. In a recent article entitled
"SYNC: The Emerging Science of Spontaneous Order," he
speaks of many systems exhibiting spontaneous synchrony,
such as birds, fish and crickets. Also included are fireflies,
some of whom light-up in unison; heart cells that beat in
synchrony, and even inanimate systems—lasers, electrical
grids, clock pendulums, quantum mechanics, and the flow
of automobile traffic.

To recall the influence that one person can have, we need only remember that modern history was crucially shaped by one person who triggered World War I in assassinating Archduke Francis Ferdinand, heir to the throne of the Austro-Hungarian Empire.

"Independence, that's middle class blasphemy. We are all dependent on one another, every soul of us on earth." George Bernard Shaw

According to scientist Gregg Braden, deep within the molecules of life there is evidence of a unifying core that shows that we are related, not only to one another, but to life in all of its forms. It is important that such a powerful message of unity is revealed at a time when nearly a third of the world's nations are engaged in armed conflict. This revelation, a powerful confirmation of human unity, may give us hope when our pervasive differences seem to be unsolvable.

We need to be reminded of this unifying factor as we struggle personally to learn to master our emotions and thoughts. Often we cause division and shatter harmony because we have allowed fear to rule our thoughts, words and decisions.

It doesn't matter whether you feel your thoughts, words, or decisions are important because the fact is that they do have a significant impact, both locally and globally. We are jointly creating our world and the outcome is in our hands and only in our hands.

"The separateness apparent in the world is secondary. Beyond that world of opposites is an unseen, but experienced unity and identity in us all." Joseph Campbell

What was the one singular defining event in your life? What individual had the most powerful effect on you in your formative years? How did this contribute to who you have become?

space

Space is derived from the Latin *spatium* and the Latin *patere*, meaning to lie open. Thus, space is boundless. We usually think we know what space is, but the soul of the word tells us that it knows no bounds and thus is beyond human comprehension or understanding.

"But how can finite grasp Infinity?" Dryden

Recently, two teams of scientists created some of the fundamental building blocks of life in a laboratory that simulates conditions found in deep space. Their work provides new evidence that the elements of life may have been delivered to earth from space.

New discoveries are being made all the time. A recent article in the *Washington Post* described the discovery of what may have been the earliest sources of light. The question of when the first light formed was addressed by religious texts for a long time before scientists could start to deal with it, said Avi Loeb of Harvard University.

"Space is the stature of God." Joubert

As we look up and stare into this deep, open space surrounding us, we can only feel and contemplate, with awe and wonder, all the many galaxies, stars, and planets that coexist with us. The sun, our solar system's life-giving star, constantly gives radiant and abundant light to all the planets, and they remain in orbital place because of an orderly universe.

Our sun doesn't separate good and evil, male and female, plants, animals, or minerals. It exemplifies and generates an infinite source of Divine light into the deep, open spaces within us and in all that exists. This creative light is the essence of who we are and of our universal connectedness. Thus, is there any reason to doubt the limitless nature of the creative power we have been given? We are forever united with the vastness of space, and although we may seem to be an infinitesimal speck in the universe, we are an essential and irreplaceable part of this infinite light.

"Man always sees the infinite shadowed forth in something finite." Thomas Carlyle

"Hold infinity in the palm of your hand." William Blake

Can you recall the feeling you experienced the first time that you looked up at the stars when you were a child? Have you recaptured the experience of space's mystery and awe recently? If not, are you inspired to do so now?

spirituality/politics

Spirituality is derived from the Latin, *spiritus,* meaning the breath of life or life of the soul itself; we speak often of Divine Spirit, Holy Spirit, or pure Spirit. Politics is derived from the Greek, *polis,* meaning the art and science of government for *polites,* or citizens.

The soul of spirituality, rooted in breath, is our "life" in totality. This holds true for citizens of all nations and tribes. Do you ever think of these two words, spirituality and politics, as having any relationship? Do you view politics as demonstrating an understanding about God and life?

These two words have been paired purposely. The roots of politics and spirituality demonstrate that since all life is spiritual and all of the concerns of everyone in life are the activity of politics, then they are inextricably bound together. The will of the majority is what we see reflected in the world. It follows that whatever is happening around us occurs within the context of our collective will.

"In our age there is no such thing as 'keeping out of politics.' All issues are political issues." George Orwell

Do you hear many people express their feelings of powerlessness in the face of life situations today? This comes from a lack of deep awareness that what each of us thinks, says, or does has real significance in a much more powerful way than we often realize. If we were to become truly conscious of this, how would our thoughts, words, and actions be different? Are you aware that if you abdicate responsibility for making informed, conscious choices, your unconscious intentions will choose for you?

We see political leaders today attempting to solve problems by changing economic and social policies, or perhaps by military action. There are times and circumstances when these measures can help to manage the effects of situations posing a threat to mankind, but what is truly needed for ultimate solutions is for hearts to be touched and changed so that real transformation can be brought to fruition. This will only happen when compassion flows freely through all of human consciousness and action.

"When you can't solve the problem, manage it." Robert Schuller

It is obvious that our world needs true leaders whose example and leadership are joined with wisdom that includes a balance of intuition and rationality; leaders who are able to envision the effects of every decision they make and who are aware of the unity of politics and spirituality. When this happens, perhaps a Department of Peace can become an effective reality in our government.

The recognition of such unity, says Richard Falk, "can build the sort of global polity that can sustain life and fulfill human potentiality, but this will not happen without the strong participation of the established world religions from East and West providing the normative frame for a unifying process that is built on a celebration of diversity."

If this is so, do you see any possibility of this happening? Do you want to be a part of helping this to happen?

Have you ever thought of the words politics or spirituality in this way? What are you supporting with your thoughts, energy, time, and money? Are you consciously looking for and choosing enlightened leaders or considering becoming one yourself? The next time you go to the polls to vote, or you are on the ballot yourself, will you think of politics as an active spirituality?

time

Time is derived from the old English *tima*, and the old Norse *timi*, meaning tide. The soul of this word tells us that we must have discovered a way to describe the regular intervals of movement by observing the ocean tides.

Was it the soul of this word that prompted Sir Walter Scott to coin the phrase, 'tide and time wait for no one'? Low and high tides originally meant low and high times, until the word *tide* evolved to its more circumscribed application, i.e., shifting waters, thus definite movement in time.

We let go of the known and step into the unknown each moment. Our life's time is a continuing and dynamic process of seasons, for we are in so many ways dependent on these cycles of life and defined by their fleeting, illusive, never to be recalled moments with their peaks and valleys.

"The only way to live is to accept each minute as an unrepeatable miracle, which is exactly what it is: a miracle and unrepeatable." Storm Jameson

The amazing phenomenon of tides causes one to reflect that each moment in time contributes to the rhythm of life. How often each day do we honor this flowing rhythm of our lives by a conscious awareness of the present? It seems that frequently we unconsciously resist this gift, fixated as many of us are on clock time and preoccupied with the past or the future.

Whenever you are waiting for someone, or for something to happen, now that you are aware of the soul of the word time, can you think of the ocean tides? Then, holding that thought, can you feel the joy and peace of the marvelous silence that exists in between each wave?

"What then is time? If no one asks me, I know what it is. If I wish to explain it to him who asks, I do not know." Saint Augustine

The teenaged Albert Einstein asked the question: "What would the world look like if I rode on a beam of light?" The earth would be frozen in time, he later figured, its clocks still, its action caught in a photograph. Out of that question came his unique Theory of Relativity in 1905. This original idea changed our understanding of how the universe works. If the speed of light is constant, then time and motion are relative to the observer.

Since the bodies we live in can cease to function and exist at any second, how to use the time we have been given is a huge conundrum that we face each day. Each moment we have to set priorities and make either a conscious or unconscious decision concerning time and how to use it wisely and responsibly.

Poet Naomi Nye writes, "Walk around feeling like a leaf. Know you could tumble any second. Then decide what to do with your time."

The Buddhist monk Lobsang Samten, a former personal attendant to the Dalai Lama, spoke of the 'lesson of impermanence' to author Jane Bay while journeying to Tibet. On the way, they witnessed a cremation and the monk commented, "At every moment you are dying and everything and everyone else is also rising and passing away." His words made her aware of the 'now' moment in time, and how important it is to be fully present in that moment, for it is all that we truly have!

"Time is our destiny. Time is our hope. Time is our despair. And time is the mirror in which we see eternity. Let me point to three of the many mysteries of time: its power to devour anything within its sphere; its power to receive eternity within itself; and its power to drive toward an ultimate end, a new creation." Paul Tillich

Would you agree that time is the most valuable treasure we have for ourselves and that we share with others?

Are love, compassion and reverence dominant in what Tillich calls the power that your time allows you to bring forth 'new creations'?

AFTERWORD

"In the beginning was the Word." *The Hidden Souls of Words* returns us to this beginning and shows us how important it is to understand the spiritual power of words and the initial impulse behind the thoughts that each word represents. We need to acknowledge that for as long as human civilization continues, we will never have words adequate to express the spiritual. From the reading of this book, you have embraced the true heart-felt significance of many words you use on a daily basis. Perhaps this will inspire you to share not only these word souls, but to look for the souls of other words that are important to you to ensure that you are truly communicating your intentions.

Humanity has suffered wars, famine, depression, death, and destruction that have stemmed in large part from the improper understanding and use of our words. This horrifying legacy has been the basis of our planetary history, both ancient and modern. Through inspiration, innovation and education, mankind can and must create true spiritual communication in both the spoken and written word.

As we share the deeper meaning of these words, we will bring healing to our personal relationships and to the world in general. In this way, a new day will dawn where our words touch all hearts and souls as well as minds. The discord and strife we have undergone as a people, culture, and world will be alleviated.

We can experience this in our daily lives by taking time to explore and put into practice the authentic meanings that the souls of the words in this book convey. One method is to pause, become still and take a moment to reflect before entering into any kind of exchange with another. Then we can proceed to come from the peaceful presence beyond thought that is, in truth, our essence and connection to the infinite. Our words will then carry the true intention underlying our rational thoughts into all of our communications.

The soul of this book and its profound objective is to highlight the need for a dramatic change in our knowledge and use of language. A new way of thinking—one that expresses our fundamental unity and heartfelt concern for one another—is calling out to be established. Can we break free of our ancient mindsets and dare to embark together to create a more conscious use of language based on these principles? I say indeed we can!

Using the revelations in this book will enable us to take a giant step in this direction. Our world will transform only as we change individually. These changes will lead to the societal transformation that is so desperately needed. Science has established that we live in a holographic universe where the energy form of the whole is contained in every tiny particle, and every particle contains the energy form of the whole. As Marcus Aurelius said, "All living things are inter-woven, each with the other."

This book is a clarion call to humanity to create more accepting, effective, loving and peaceful communications. We need to turn this key to open the door to a world of har-mony—a harmony that arises out of our diverse cultures, opinions and beliefs.

You may be wondering how you as an individual can make a significant contribution to such a monumental undertaking—you might even think this is an impossible dream and task. But you can make this a living reality and not just another theory expounded for intellectual stimula-tion. And the singular, unique contribution of your innate gifts is essential. How you play your part affects the whole. You can be the crucial link that sets off the chain reaction that culminates in a necessary global transformation. Your response can literally be a matter of life or death for all of us.

What if we imagined the world as we know it could be—a safe place to live, work, and raise our children in a loving, healthy and supportive environment? The power of our words will create this reality when we choose to use our words as instruments to facilitate this higher purpose. Envision children who understand the intrinsic wisdom of their own minds and how they can integrate that power with rational negotiation, personal responsibility, and initiatives that serve others. Think what peace and productivity would result if this happened in our businesses, corporations, and especially governments.

As we realize that our focused attention—whether work-ing alone or in concert with others—is our tool of creation, we can see what our divergent fragmented attentions and intentions have produced. Looking at our world today, it is obvious that our collective focus has not been based on our collective Divine nature. When we remember to focus from the place of absolute love, miracles can then be an everyday occurrence for all of us.

The Hidden Souls of Words is a prayer from my heart to your heart. May the power and spirit of the word souls in this book inspire you to bring about this magnificent, transformational possibility. Rest in the assurance that the Infinite Light radiates within you, everyone and everything regardless of any situation life may present. May all of us grow in the knowledge that this unifying Light is our true home and freedom.